Action Against Small Arms

A Resource and Training Handbook

International Alert, Oxfam GB, and Saferworld

International Alert is a UK-based non-government organisation, committed to the just and peaceful transformation of violent conflicts. It works with partner organisations to identify and address the root causes of conflicts and to conduct research on the control of light weapons, security-sector reform, the role of the private sector, the impact of development, and women's contribution to peace-building. Alert seeks to influence practice and policies at all levels, bringing into the policy arena the voices of those most affected by conflict.

www.international-alert.org

Oxfam GB, founded in 1942, is a development, humanitarian, and campaigning agency dedicated to finding lasting solutions to poverty and suffering around the world. Oxfam believes that every human being is entitled to a life of dignity and opportunity, and it works with others worldwide to make this become a reality.

Oxfam GB is a member of Oxfam International, a confederation of 12 agencies of diverse cultures and languages, which share a commitment to working for an end to injustice and poverty – both in long-term development work and at times of crisis.

www.oxfam.org.uk
www.oxfam.org.uk/publications

Saferworld is an independent non-government organisation working to identify, develop, and publicise more effective approaches to tackling and preventing armed conflicts. Its Arms Programme aims to foster greater international restraint over transfers of arms; at the same time, it aims to work with governments and civil society on the ground in regions of conflict, to better control the flows of arms and to reduce demand for them.

www.saferworld.org.uk

Action Against Small Arms

A Resource and Training Handbook

Jim Coe and Henry Smith

Practical Action Publishing Ltd
25 Albert Street, Rugby, CV21 2SD, Warwickshire, UK
www.practicalactionpublishing.com

First published by International Alert, Oxfam GB, and Saferworld in 2003
Reprinted by Practical Action Publishing

Oxfam GB is registered as a charity in England and Wales (no. 202918) and Scotland (SCO 039042).
Oxfam GB is a member of Oxfam International.

Paperback ISBN: 9780855984977
PDF ISBN: 9780855986490

A catalogue record for this publication is available from the British Library.

The manufacturer's authorised representative in the EU for product safety is
Lightning Source France, 1 Av. Johannes Gutenberg, 78310 Maurepas, France.
compliance@lightningsource.fr

Contents

List of figures

List of tables

Preface

'The rebels had threatened to kill the boys for hiding in a tree during an early morning attack on the village. The mother asked that she be killed instead. In her presence, one of the boys was asked to pull the trigger against his mother; he refused and was shot in the leg. The younger child was then asked to shoot his mother, and he did so. He was conscripted as a hard, fearless fighter.

'The attack on the city of Freetown saw the death of more than 5000 people. Vultures continuously fed on human bodies, as there were no people to bury the dead. People were pressed at gunpoint into houses, which were sprayed with petrol and set on fire. Whoever tried to escape was immediately shot.'[1]
Issac Lappia – Amnesty International, Sierra Leone

In recent years, campaigns against landmines, for debt relief and for an International Criminal Court have demonstrated the extraordinary capacity of ordinary people to band together behind a cause and fundamentally change the policies of governments. Surely, the illicit trade in small arms and light weapons deserves similar attention.[2]
UN Secretary General, Kofi Annan

The uncontrolled spread and misuse of small arms and light weapons (SALW) is a global problem which results in the deaths of hundreds of thousands of men, women, and children every year. Factors driving demand for these weapons include poverty, underdevelopment, the abuse of human rights, crime, conflict, and competition for resources. It is estimated that there are more than 639 million small arms and light weapons in circulation[3] around the world. More than 1000 companies are involved in the production of small arms, and at least 98 countries have the capacity to produce such weapons and ammunition for them.

The global trade in small arms is huge: its value is estimated to exceed US$ 335 million – and it involves governments, companies, and individuals from around the world.[4] The human cost of the proliferation and misuse of small arms and light weapons is impossible to estimate. It destroys lives, intensifies and prolongs conflict, kills and injures. Millions of people are forced to flee their homes. The Secretary General of the United Nations, Kofi Annan, speaking in 2001, declared:

> *Small arms ...exacerbate conflict, spark refugee flows, undermine the rule of law, and spawn a culture of violence and impunity. In short, small arms are a threat to peace and development, to democracy and human rights.*[5]

Representatives of civil society – journalists, non-government organisations, community groups, religious organisations, and academics – are committed to acting to reduce the catastrophic impact of small arms and light weapons. International initiatives such as the UN Programme of Action on Small Arms and Light Weapons have been developed partly as a consequence of concerted action by civil society at all levels. And around the world, in conflict-affected regions and cities threatened by violent crime, and in countries that dominate SALW production and export markets, organisations and individuals are working for change. However, this work is undermined by the failure of governments to prevent the proliferation, availability, and misuse of the weapons.

This manual aims to help civil-society organisations and others to persuade governments and others to take positive action to address the problem. It is based on the experiences and expertise of people around the world who have taken practical, imaginative action on the issues. The book consists of four parts:

Part 1: The policy context
Part 2: Planning for action
Part 3: Taking action
Part 4: Contacts

The book is intended to be used in two primary ways:

- as a resource for individuals and organisations seeking to develop a programme of action; and
- as a training and resource guide for organisers of planning or training workshops.

It offers a set of sequential steps to help the user to understand SALW-related issues, to select the appropriate course of action, and to act with maximum impact. Alternatively, its separate elements may be used selectively to complement existing skills and experience.

Each part of the handbook is divided into separate stand-alone sections. Part 1 aims to provide a thorough introduction to the issues. Parts 2 and 3, which are illustrated with examples, are designed to be used to enhance planning and action on a range of social-justice issues. However, representing the experiences and knowledge of all those working on SALW is impossible in a single publication, so Part 4 provides the details of organisations featured in the handbook and also addresses of others who can provide more detailed support and information upon request.

Acknowledgements

This manual is based on the experiences and opinions of individuals and organisations working to combat the proliferation of small arms and light weapons in a wide range of countries around the world. It was researched and written over a period of 18 months, involving consultations with more than 112 civil-society organisations from 41 countries. The consultations took place at the UN Conference on Small Arms and Light Weapons in New York ,and at the conference of the Humanitarian Coalition on Small Arms and Light Weapons in Nairobi, Kenya in 2001; at workshops for non-government organisations from South Asia in India, from east and west Africa in Kenya and Senegal respectively, in the Philippines, the Balkans, and Central and Eastern Europe in 2002, and in Kosovo in 2003.

The manual features case studies based on the experiences of organisations which have developed effective programmes of action to address the problems of small arms. The authors and publishers are grateful to them all for their contributions. Details of how to contact them appear in Part 4 of the manual, along with addresses of many other organisations with expertise in campaigning against small arms and light weapons.

Thanks are due also to the following for their input to the process of drafting and reviewing the text:

Oliver Sprague at Oxfam

Michael Crowley at the Arias Foundation

David Norman

Andy McLean, Liz Kirkham, Roy Isbister, Angus Urquhart, Helen Hughes, and Catherine Flew at Saferworld

Helena Vasquez , Michael Page, Lindsay Alexander, Stephanie Powell, Sarah Meek and Eugenia Piza-Lopez at International Alert

Sally Joss at IANSA.

The following organisations took part in consultations throughout the development of the manual and generously contributed time, insights, and experiences:

Academia Catavencu Press Monitoring Agency
Advocates Without Borders
Africa Peace Forum
Africa Strategic and Peace Research Group (AFSTRAG)
African Centre for Human Security (ACHUS)
African Security, Dialogue and Research
AKBKAYAN! Citizens Action Party
ALTERNAG
Alternative Planning Initiative
Amnesty International, International Secretariat
Amnesty International Czech Republic
Amnesty International India
Amnesty International Indonesia
Amnesty International Lithuania
Amnesty International Nepal
Amnesty International New Zealand
Amnesty International Philippines
Amnesty International Poland
Amnesty International Slovakia
Amnesty International Slovenia
Anti War Campaign (ARK)
Arias Foundation
Association des Femmes pour les Initiatives de Paix (AFIP)
Association des Femmes pour la Paix en Casamance (KONKETOR)
Association for Democratic Initiatives
Balkan Youth Action
Black Sea Law Community
Bulgarian Red Cross
Campaign for Conscientious Objectors
Campaign for Good Governance (CGG)
Catholic Justice and Peace Commission
Center for Peace and Economic Empowerment
Centre for Anti-War Action
Centre for Conflict Resolution (GANSA)
Centre for Democracy and Development (CDD)
Centre for Democratic Empowerment (CEDE)
Centre for New Visions
Centre for Peace Studies
Centre for the Study of Democracy
CERES
Coalition Nationale de la société civile pour la lutte contre la proliferation des armes légères
Collectif Cadres Casamance
Commission Nationale du Senegal
Croatian Helsinki Committee
Ecumenical Commission for Displaced Families and Communities (ECDFC)
Enseignante CESTI
European Institute for Risk, Security and Communication
Families of Victims of Involuntary Disappearances
Far Eastern University
Forum-Centre for Strategic Research and Documentation
Forumi i Iniciativs Qytetare (FIQ)
Foundation for Security and Development in Africa (FOSDA)
Foundation Help
GZO Peace Institute
HANDICAP International
Human Rights Watch
IANSA
Institute for Security Studies
Institute of War and Peace Reporting

Isiolo Peace Committee
Journalists for Children and Women's Rights and Protection of Environment
Kenya Coalition Against Landmines
Kosovo Youth Council
Liberia Women's Initiative
Lithuanian Center for Human Rights
Lithuanian Red Cross
Local Democracy Agency
Media Against Conflict
Media Flash
Medical Action Group
MOST (Youth Organisation)
Mouvement contre les armes légères en Afrique d'Ouest (MALAO)
Mouvement des Femmes de la Mano River
Movement for Disarmament
NESEHNUTI-Brno
Non-Violence International
Pastoralist Peace and Development Initiative
PCBM
Peace Advocates Zamboanga/Commission on Human Rights
People for Peace
People in Need
People in Peril Association
People with Disabilities
Philippines Human Rights Information Center
Philippines Trial Lawyers Association
Polish Red Cross
Prague Indymedia Centre
PREDA
RADDHO
Republika Srpska Red Cross
Réseau des Journalistes pour la Paix et l'Intégration (RJPI)
SaferAfrica
Safer-Albania
SALIGAD
Security Research and Information Centre
SEESAC
Slovak Working Group on Arms
Societas 2001
Soros Foundation
Sudan Programme
Szeged Center for Security Policy
TARA
Task Forces Detainees of the Philippines
The Women's Journalists League of Albania
Transparency International
UNDP
UNREC
UP Third World Studies Centre
West African Network for Peacebuilding (WANEP)
Women Forum Montenegro
Women's Centre for Peace and Development (WOPED)
Young Moros Professionals/Al Mujadillah Foundation
Yugoslav Red Cross
'ZaMen' Magazine

Abbreviations and acronyms

ATT: Arms Trade Treaty
BASIC: British American Security Information Council
CEDE: Centre for Democratic Empowerment
COIB: Conscientious Objectors in Bosnia
DDR: disarmament, demobilisation, and reintegration
DRP: demobilisation and reintegration programme
ECOSOC: Economic and Social Council
ECOWAS: Economic Community of West African States
EU: European Union
FIQ: Forumi I Iniciativs Qytetare
FOSDA: Foundation for Security and Development in Africa
IANSA: International Action Network on Small Arms
ICBL: International Campaign to Ban Landmines
KYPPEDE: Kibera Youth Programme for Peace and Development
LPO: licensed production overseas
MALAO: Mouvement Contre les Armes Légères in Afrique de l'Oest
NISAT: Norwegian Initiative on Small Arms Transfers
OAS: Organisation of American States
OAU: Organisation of African Unity (now African Union)
OSCE: Organisation for Security and Co-operation in Europe
PoA: UN Programme of Action to Prevent, Combat, and Eradicate the Illicit Trade in Small Arms and Light Weapons in All its Aspects
PPDI: Pastoralist Peace and Development Initiative
SADC: Southern African Development Community
SALW: small arms and light weapons
SIPRI: Stockholm International Peace Research Institute
SSRP: security sector reform programme
SWOT: strengths, weaknesses, opportunities, threats
UKWG: United Kingdom Working Group on Arms
UNDDA: United Nations Department of Disarmament Affairs
UNDIR: United Nations Institute for Disarmament Research

Part 1

The policy context

Contents

Introduction

Part 1 of the handbook analyses the effects of the proliferation and misuse of small arms and light weapons (SALW). It introduces the range of measures that are needed to address the problems relating to their supply and demand, and reviews the key regional, multilateral, and international initiatives currently in place to address these problems.

Section 1: Definitions and statistics

This section introduces some of the key elements of the problem, illustrating them with relevant statistics. It outlines the United Nations' definition of SALW and lists the major categories covered by the definition. It defines the nature of small-arms transfers and suggests a definition to describe 'illicit' and 'licit' transfers.

Section 2: The effects of small arms and light weapons

This section analyses the effects of the proliferation and misuse of SALW in terms of the following:

- abuses of human rights and breaches of international humanitarian law
- the 'War on Terrorism'
- cultures of violence
- violent crime
- gender
- development.

Section 3: Recommended measures to address the proliferation and misuse of small arms and light weapons

This section analyses the range of measures that are needed to address the problem. It first identifies measures to reduce the demand for SALW and concludes by reviewing the measures needed to control their production and transfer.

Measures to address demand

- weapons collection and disarmament, demobilisation, and reintegration (DDR) programmes
- regulating civilian ownership of SALW
- SALW and reform of the security sector
- private military and security companies and the proliferation and misuse of SALW
- management of stockpiles and surplus weapons.

Measures to control supply and transfer

- express prohibitions
- restrictions based on use
- areas of emerging international consensus
- establishing a normative framework
- establishing effective operative procedures
- licensing controls and procedures
- end-use certification and monitoring
- marking and tracing
- controlling the activities of brokering and shipping agents
- controlling licensed production overseas.

Section 4: Existing initiatives to address the proliferation and misuse of SALW

This section introduces and analyses some of the major international and regional agreements and initiatives that exist to control the proliferation and misuse of SALW. Each example has been selected for three reasons. Firstly that it has made a contribution to the development of other initiatives and action: for instance the Bamako Declaration was important in the development of sub-regional initiatives such as the Nairobi Declaration and as a stepping stone to international action such as the UN Programme of Action on SALW. Secondly that it represents a specific type of initiative – in terms of geographical coverage or scope of content. And finally because it represents good opportunities for the engagement of civil society.

This section begins with an analysis of the 2001 UN Small Arms Conference, the resultant Programme of Action, and the UN small-arms process. It then introduces the UN Firearms Protocol and the Wassenaar Arrangement. Finally, this section covers some of the key regional and inter-regional initiatives and agreements. However, it does not present a complete overview of all regional initiatives; there have been moves towards action in regions not covered in this section. The following initiatives are included:

- The Bamako Declaration on the African Common Position on the Illicit Proliferation, Circulation and Trafficking of Small Arms and Light Weapons
- The Nairobi Declaration
- The SADC Protocol on the Control of Firearms, Ammunition, and Other Related Materials
- The ECOWAS Moratorium on the Import, Export and Manufacture of Small Arms and Light Weapons in Africa
- The Inter-American Convention against the Illicit Manufacturing of and Trafficking in Firearms, Ammunition, Explosives and Other Related Materials
- OSCE Document on Small Arms
- The EU Code of Conduct on Arms Exports
- The EU Joint Action on Small Arms

1 Definitions and statistics

What are small arms and light weapons?

Although there is no universally accepted classification of these weapons, a report by a UN panel of experts in 1997 contained the most commonly used definition.[1] *Light weapons* is a generic term which is used to cover a range of weapons portable by man, animal, or machine – from revolvers and machine guns to anti-tank and anti-aircraft missile systems. *Small arms* are a sub-set of the category of light weapons which includes only those weapons that can be fired, maintained, and transported by one person. In this handbook, small arms, light weapons, firearms, and weapons are generally referred to as *SALW*. Furthermore, unless the context dictates otherwise, no distinction is made between commercial firearms (such as hunting rifles) and small arms and light weapons designed for military use (such as assault rifles).

Table 1: Definitions

Small arms include:	revolvers self-loading pistols rifles and carbines sub-machine guns assault rifles light machine-guns
Light weapons include the above, as well as:	heavy machine-guns grenade launchers portable anti-aircraft guns portable anti-tank guns recoilless rifles portable launchers of anti-tank missile and rocket systems portable launchers of anti-aircraft missile systems mortars of calibres of less than 100 mm
Ammunition and explosives for small arms and light weapons include:	cartridges (rounds) for small arms shells and missiles for light weapons anti-personnel and anti-tank hand grenades landmines, explosives, munitions for single-action anti-aircraft and anti-tank systems

How many small arms are there?

According to the Small Arms Survey (*Counting the Human Cost*, 2002), there are estimated to be 639 million small arms and light weapons (SALW) currently in circulation around the world.[2] Perhaps surprisingly, civilian possession accounts for almost two thirds of the global total, with at least 378 million firearms in private hands.

Table 2: Distribution of known global small arms[3]

Ownership group	Numbers held	Percentage of total
State-owned: combined tota	259,600,000	40.6
Armed forces	*(241,600,000)*	*(37.8)*
Police forces	*(18,000,00)*	*(2.8)*
Civilian possession	370,300,000	59.2
Rebel groups	1,000,000	0.2
TOTAL	638,900,000	100

In addition to existing small arms and light weapons, new small arms are being manufactured, sold, transferred, and transported every day.

Box 1: Where do small arms come from, and who owns them?[4]

More than 1,000 companies worldwide are involved in some aspect of small-arms production.

At least 98 countries produce, or have the capacity to produce, small arms and/or ammunition.

Thirteen countries dominate the global market for small arms. They are Austria, Belgium, Brazil, China, France, Germany, Israel, Italy, Russian Federation, Spain, Switzerland, the United Kingdom, and the United States of America.

The total value of global small-arms production, including ammunition, in 2000 was at least $7.4 billion.

What are SALW transfers?[5]

The definition of an arms transfer is relatively simple. A transfer is the *reallocation of small arms from the possession of one actor to another.* There are always at least two principal actors involved in any transfer, namely the originator and the recipient. These actors can be individuals, groups such as companies or armed opposition groups, criminal organisations, or States. However, other actors, such as arms brokering and transportation agents, are also often involved in facilitating transfers.

In general there are three main types of small-arms transfer:

- **'Legal' transfers**: These occur with either the active or passive involvement of governments or their authorised agents, and in accordance with both national and international law. However, where the end use of the weapons transfers is in contravention of national and/or international law, then the transfer becomes illicit.
- **'Illegal' transfers**: These are in clear violation of national and/or international laws such as United Nations arms embargoes. Without official government consent or control, these transfers may involve false or forged paperwork, or corrupt government officials acting on their own for personal gain.
- **'Grey-market' transfers**: These are often the most problematic to define, because they are neither unarguably legal nor clearly illegal but may contain elements of both definitions. For example, a transfer of weapons that eventually reaches a destination covered by a UN arms embargo may have started its journey as part of a legal State-sanctioned deal, but it has been diverted from its stated destination during the export stage. Grey-market transfers often involve governments, their agents, or individuals exploiting loopholes or unintentionally circumventing national controls.

Some have sought to define such transactions as 'illicit', although there is no international legal definition of the term. However, international consensus is starting to emerge on this issue. For example, the UN Conference on Disarmament has itself put forward a wider definition of the illicit trade in conventional arms, which includes 'that international trade in conventional arms, which is contrary to the laws of states and/or international law'.[6] Many non-government organisations (NGOs) have argued that those weapons that are transferred and used in violation of international legal norms should also be considered illicit.

Although certain governments believe that international action on the proliferation and misuse of small arms should be restricted solely to combating the illicit trade, without consideration of the State-sanctioned trade, many in the international community believe that this narrow approach is insufficient for tackling the problem, for two reasons. Firstly, numerous studies have shown that arms from State-sanctioned transfers (or the 'legal' trade) have been diverted into illicit markets, fuelling crime, terrorism, and the trafficking of illegal drugs. In order to effectively combat the illicit trade in small arms and light weapons, it is also important to implement strategies to control the State-sanctioned trade.

Secondly, although some governments have defined the illicit trade as covering only those transfers that were not sanctioned by the exporting or recipient State, many governments and civil-society actors believe that this definition is too narrow, since it does not take into account the legality of the ultimate use of the weapons.

Indeed, years of research by NGOs and the UN have shown that some small arms and light weapons legally exported by States have ultimately been used to violate international law, through their use in violations of human rights, and breaches of international humanitarian law, by fuelling conflict and violent crime, and undermining democratic governments.

The differing interpretations of the definition of the illicit small-arms trade came to a head as the international community began to make preparations to deal with small arms at the global level for the first time, at the UN Conference on the Illicit Trade in Small Arms and Light Weapons in All Its Aspects in 2001. In an attempt to reconcile these differing interpretations, the international community agreed that the conference would seek to 'prevent, combat and eradicate the illicit trade in small arms and light weapons in all its aspects'.

2 The effects of small arms and light weapons

Small arms are used to kill and injure civilians and combatants alike. They are used in the commission of rape and other forms of sexual violence, to harass and intimidate, and to perpetrate other violent crimes; and they undermine the effects of post-conflict reconstruction and development. The problem of small-arms proliferation and misuse manifests itself in different ways in different places, and the causes and effects of this problem sometimes differ, depending on the context in which they are used.

Small arms facilitating conflict, human-rights abuses, and breaches of international humanitarian law[7]

The growing availability of small arms has been associated with the increased incidence of internal conflicts.[8] While accumulations of small arms may not alone create the conflicts in which they are used, their availability intensifies conflicts by increasing the lethality and duration of violence, and by increasing the sense of insecurity which leads to a greater demand for weapons.[9] Some commentators consider the easy availability of small arms to be a 'proximate cause' of armed conflict, transforming a potentially violent situation into a full-scale conflict.[10] While small arms are frequently associated with armed conflict, arms-related violations occur in many other contexts. These violations are especially prevalent as a result of post-conflict insecurity, crime and banditry, and the militarisation of refugee camps and camps for internally displaced persons (IDPs).

The presence of small arms aggravates patterns of forced displacement. With AK-47s in hand, for instance, bandits and criminals who in the past may have carried out livestock raids and looting in pastoral communities have resorted to increased levels of violence, including the use of systematic rape and killing, to drive people from their homes and communities. Not only are communities displaced by such violence directly threatened with death and injury, but the on-going threat of violence from the availability of weapons obstructs their access to food, shelter, health care, education, and other basic services.[11]

Indeed, the militarisation of refugee and IDP camps has become a serious problem for the international community. 'Safe havens' created to aid victims of war have instead become breeding grounds for armed groups. The insecurity in the camps may pose a threat to regional stability, as camps become marketplaces for arms that fuel civil wars, crime, and terrorism.[12]

Civilians have become the deliberate targets of violence involving small arms during armed conflict. Such violence against civilians and non-combatants in situations of armed conflict is completely at odds with internationally recognised legal protections granted to non-combatants under international human-rights conventions and humanitarian law.[13] Despite these legal protections, a disproportionately high percentage of small-arms casualties in war-time are civilians. A study in Croatia, for instance, determined that civilian deaths may have accounted for up to 64 per cent of the 4,339 fatalities surveyed during the war in 1991-92.[14] Another study reported that at least 34 per cent of patients in field hospitals established by the International Committee of the Red Cross (ICRC) in Afghanistan, Rwanda, Chechnya, and the border regions of Kenya and Cambodia were civilians wounded by bullets.[15] Surveys carried out in Sierra Leone showed that almost 60 per cent of all war injuries were gunshot-related, that 11 per cent of all victims were under the age of 15, and that 43 per cent were women.[16]

Due to their increasing availability, small arms play a critical role in many abuses against personal dignity. Small arms are used to perpetrate an entire range of human-rights abuses, including rape, enforced disappearance, torture, forced displacement, and forced recruitment of children soldiers. Even in genocidal conflicts, where people have been hacked to death with machetes or other non-ballistic instruments, the victims are often initially rounded up with firearms. Heavily armed individuals create an environment in which atrocities can be committed at will by various other means. An increase in expenditure on SALW by governments in response to deteriorating security conditions may divert scarce resources away from expenditure on health care, education, and other support for economic, social, and cultural rights.

Children, especially, are victims of human-rights violations that result from the availability and misuse of small arms. UNICEF estimates that two million children were killed in armed conflict in the 1990s, many by small arms and light weapons.[17] An estimated 300,000 children under the age of 18 are exploited as soldiers in armed conflicts.[18] The simplicity of use of small arms turns even young children into deadly killers. A 19-year-old soldier in northern Uganda testified: '*I especially know how to use an AK-47 twelve-inch, which I could dismantle in less than one minute. When I turned 12 they gave me an RPG (Rocket Propelled Grenade), because I had proved myself in battle.*'[19]

Besides being killed and injured by firearms, children are often affected by the secondary costs of armed violence, including malnutrition, disease, and preventable illness.[20]

Violence involving small arms has also had a devastating impact on the humanitarian aid community. Humanitarian workers, including UN civilian staff members, are increasingly at risk as targets of firearms-related violence including killings, hostage-taking, sexual assault, armed robbery, and arbitrary arrest and detention. The UN reported that 185 civilian staff members died between 1992 and 2000, most from firearms-related violence.[21] Under threat of violence from armed militias, humanitarian agencies are often forced to surrender goods and materials that were intended for aid operations. Increasing threats to staff members have resulted in an increased focus on human security in UN field operations.

The UN Conference to Prevent, Combat and Eradicate the Illicit Trade in Small Arms and Light Weapons in All its Aspects was the first occasion when the international community came together to discuss the global crisis caused by the proliferation and misuse of these weapons. However, one major failing of the conference was the inadequate consideration given to the impact of SALW on human rights and international humanitarian law. Despite this, these two important topics are now being given increasing attention by governments, NGOs, intergovernment organisations, and UN agencies and structures. The devastating role of SALW in perpetrating human-rights abuses and breaches of international humanitarian law is highlighted in the following testimony from Afghanistan.

> *'First they [Taleban fighters] rounded up the people in the streets. They then went from house to house and arrested the men of the families, except for the very old men. Nothing could stop them, and they did not spare any of the houses. In one house, the mother of a young man whom the Taleban were taking away held on to him, saying she would not allow him to go away without her. The Taleban began to hit the woman brutally with their rifle butts. She died. They took away the son and shot him dead. They were our neighbours. When they arrested the people, they tied their hands behind their back and took them away. They took them to areas behind Bazar Kona and fired at them. They executed a lot of people.'*[22]

Small-arms controls and the 'War on Terrorism'

Extensive evidence gathered by law-enforcement agencies, journalists, NGOs, and the UN has shown how weaknesses in national, regional, and international arms controls have been exploited by arms brokers and irresponsible governments to facilitate the transfer of arms, including SALW, to criminals, human-rights violators, and terrorists.

Since the attacks on the World Trade Center and the Pentagon in the USA on 11 September 2001, many arms-control experts have called for stricter controls on small-arms transfers as a crucial element in the international community's strategy to combat al-Qa'eda and other terrorist organisations. States should now be strengthening SALW controls and providing greater resources for their enforcement. Although certain initiatives in this regard have been taken, a number of leading arms-exporting States are actually relaxing controls on sales of arms to other State and non-State actors. This can be seen with regard to US policy.

According to NGO analysts, since 11 September 2001 the US government has requested nearly $3.8 billion in security assistance and related aid for 67 countries allegedly involved in some way in the 'War on Terrorism'.[23] Of the countries currently selected to receive US military aid, 32 were named in the US State Department's 2000 human-rights report as having human-rights records that were 'poor' or worse.[24]

Box 2: A cause for concern: arming the Philippines Army?[25]

Since the terrorist attacks of September 11th 2001, the US government has increased its military support to the government of the Philippines. According to US government documents, this support has included excess military equipment, including 30,000 M16 rifles. The US government is also providing increased military training to counter terrorist threats, and to fight various armed militant and kidnap-for-ransom groups that are believed by the US government to have links with terrorist organisations such as al-Qa'eda. The military assistance continues, despite US government reports of human-rights violations by members of the Philippine government armed forces. Many NGOs are concerned that the arms and training are given without incorporating rigorous human-rights safeguards or proper vetting of units receiving weapons and training under existing US law. The Philippines receives substantial small-arms supplies from the USA, Canada, and South Africa, and is reportedly saturated with small arms. An escalation of armed conflict in Mindanao in 2000 led to the displacement of more than 500,000 civilians, amid reports of indiscriminate bombings and human-rights violations. In February 2003, a further peak of conflict resulted in the displacement of more than 150,000 people. It is clear that increased US military assistance to the Philippines at this time risks intensifying patterns of human-rights violations and so aggravating local tensions and prolonging the conflict, unless accompanied by strong measures to ensure that the basic rights of civilians are protected.

Box 3: Arms to Afghanistan[26]

The small-arms trade has fuelled on-going, devastating war in Afghanistan for 23 years. The US government, via its Central Intelligence Agency (CIA), gave large quantities of light weapons to Mujahideen groups in Afghanistan resisting the Soviet invasion and occupation between 1979 and 1989, despite the fact that thousands of Afghan civilians were deliberately and arbitrarily killed by warring Mujahideen fighters, who were also responsible for widespread beatings, abductions, and rapes. In 2001, US forces in Afghanistan were attacked with Stinger missile systems, supplied by the USA in the 1980s. Other foreign powers, including Pakistan, Iran, and China, also supplied munitions to the Mujahideen groups, who also captured arms from troops of the former Soviet Union.

The Taleban were also armed originally by the USA and Pakistan. By late 2001, the weapons markets in Taleban-held towns and villages on the Afghan borders with Pakistan and Iran were some of the most deadly arms bazaars in the world and were still reportadly doing a heavy trade in arms, including missiles originating in the USA and elsewhere, and Kalashnikovs made under licence in China and Egypt.

Osama bin Laden reportedly spent several years in the early 1980s fighting alongside Mujahideen against Soviet forces in Afghanistan, and setting up military training camps there for foreign, including Arab, recruits. In a 2001 criminal trial of al-Qa'eda members convicted of bombing two US embassies in Africa, Essam al Ridi testified that he had bought 25 US sniper rifles from a US company and shipped them to Afghanistan in the late 1980s. The rifles are capable of shooting down helicopters, piercing armour, or destroying fuel tanks from long distances. (The US State Department no longer allows the commercial export of these weapons to individuals.) In June 2001, there were reports that bin Laden's followers had bought missiles and small arms from dealers in Peshawar, and had flown in extra recruits and supplies to a camp south-west of Kandahar. US and Afghan troops in 2003 continue to engage with well-armed Taleban and al-Qa'eda fighters in the south, who threaten to destabilise the current political process and have halted effective delivery of humanitarian aid in the area.

The examples in the boxes illustrate clearly the dangers of supplying arms to government and non-government actors who have little regard for human rights and international humanitarian law. While the potential for such arms to be used to commit serious violations is clear, supplier governments are often powerless to prevent the resale of arms by unscrupulous regimes and insurgent groups to terrorists and others who pose a serious risk to international peace and security.

Small arms and cultures of violence

The proliferation and increasing availability of small arms and light weapons in many regions of the world encourage and perpetuate so-called 'cultures of violence', whereby traditional mechanisms of conflict resolution are eroded and the use of guns emerges as a norm within society. This is particularly the case in post-conflict States, where weapons remain in circulation and State security is weak or absent, leading to a reliance on weapons as a means of self-defence, with resultant increases in violence at the community level and a further erosion of human security.

Cultures of violence may also emerge in polarised societies where certain groups use violence as a consequence of, or reaction to, their oppression and marginalisation. The gang culture that exists in areas of the United States and Brazil, for example, represents a social context within which the use of violence is endemic, and where guns may come to be seen as a symbol of power and masculinity, a perception strengthened by the glamorous portrayal of guns in the media. This further polarises power relations among races, classes, and sexes and creates a demand for weapons that is met both legally and illicitly.[27]

Box 4: Cultures of violence in South Africa

Apartheid in South Africa, the violent struggle against it, and the political transition that followed left a legacy of poverty and inequality. Widespread unemployment, appalling living conditions in shanty towns, and gender-based violence contribute to high levels of crime. Children are among those who become both victims and perpetrators of a cycle of violence and fear. South Africa has the highest murder rate in the world and also faces an increasing threat from HIV. According to the Institute of Security Studies, 'in 12 years' time you'll have at least a quarter of a million orphans, with no role models to guide them. They won't care less, because they are infected with HIV. They will have access to guns ... the escalation of violence could be so great that it becomes the only determinant of whether life is worth living or not.'[28]

Small arms and violent crime

The easy availability of small arms and light weapons fuels the activities of criminal groups and terrorist organisations around the world. The possession of such weapons allows them to carry out their operations through threats and violence and to protect their interests against both rivals and State law enforcers. The illicit sale, use, and trafficking of SALW thus constitutes a major social problem for many countries and regions. In Central America, for example, estimates of the number of illegal weapons in the hands of civilians range from two million for the entire region to two million in Guatemala alone. The homicide rate in the region is approaching 60 per 100,000 population – almost double the average for the rest of the Americas.[29] Nor is the increasing use of SALW in violent crime limited to the South. Trends in much of the developed world also show an increase in the level of SALW being used in crime. In London, for example, gun-related crime rose by 11 per cent in 2002.[30] In many societies, law-enforcement agencies are struggling to deal with such crimes, with increasing numbers of victims and by-standers being shot and seriously injured or fatally wounded. A World Health Organisation report of 2001 stated that due to a lack of reliable global data it was not yet known how many of the 2.3 million violent deaths each year involve small arms, but that best estimates indicated that several hundred thousand people die each year as a result of gun-related homicides, suicides, and armed conflict.[31]

The SALW that are used in violent crime come from a wide variety of sources. In terms of the global illicit trade in SALW as a whole, few weapons begin their lives as illicit commodities, in the sense of having been manufactured and sold illicitly. However, in particular regions – such as South Asia and Central America – illicit production does make a significant contribution to the problem of illicit SALW. In societies which permit significant levels of civilian ownership of SALW – such as the United States and South Africa – most weapons used in crime are, in the first instance, manufactured and sold legally to civilians. Some such SALW are subsequently lost, stolen, illegally resold, or loaned before being used in violent crime. The illegal sale of SALW by law-enforcement officials can also contribute to the problem.[32] In societies where there are low levels of civilian firearm-ownership, criminals rely on specialised networks to bring weapons into the country and distribute them. For example, in the UK, 90 per cent of illegally owned firearms are manufactured outside the country.[33] In other societies where law and order mechanisms have broken down, looting from State arsenals has led to large quantities of SALW entering the illicit market and being used in crime. In Albania, for example, 350,000 weapons are still unaccounted for following the collapse of State authority in 1997.[34]

In many societies, former combatants and others who lack the skills or the opportunity to earn a livelihood through lawful means have retained or acquired SALW in order to pursue banditry and other forms of violent crime. Indeed, the ready availability of SALW in some post-conflict societies has led to the emergence of so-called 'war economies' – a phenomenon typical of weak, war-torn societies, including for instance Georgia, which is plagued with illegal activities. In such war economies, smuggling of arms, illegal drugs, contraband petrol, cigarettes, cars, and even people is a feature. Armed struggle has become an end in itself, since certain groups benefit from the volatile situation and the rampant proliferation of arms that goes with it. The State is powerless to resist those wanting to maintain conflict for the sake of profit, and as a result armed gangs control all aspects of social life.[35]

Box 5: Armed violence in Brazil[36]

A report on armed factions in Rio de Janeiro produced by Viva Rio and the Institute for Religious Studies found that almost four thousand people under 18 died from gun-related injuries between 1987 and 2001, and that more firearm deaths were reported in Rio than battle deaths in Colombia, Sierra Leone, Yugoslavia, Afghanistan, Uganda, and Israel. An average of 80 per cent of murders in the city are gun-related, and the number of murders has been rising since the 1970s, in parallel with an increase in the use of high-powered firearms, such as Kalashnikov AK-47s and Heckler and Koch G3s, by drug traffickers in the city.

Small arms and gender

Men and women, boys and girls have different experiences of small arms in terms of their use and impact, as well as different capacities to deal with their negative effects. Unless these differences are understood, the ability to plan and implement effective and meaningful programmes to counteract the abuse of small arms will be limited.

Whereas *sex* denotes the fixed, biological differences between men and women, *gender* represents the socialised differences. Gender impacts on men's and women's roles, relationships, experiences, and expectations in society, as well as their access to power and resources. Of course, not all men, nor all women, are the same. Men's and women's gender roles and relations will vary according to their age, ethnicity, class, culture, religion, and socio-economic status.

Although there are few statistics available that are differentiated by sex, it is a common perception that men are the predominant users of small arms, in times of both conflict and peace. In war time, young men are the primary targets for voluntary and forced conscription into State and non-State armies. In relatively stable societies, men also tend to be the primary users, or owners, of small arms in the household, at work, in crime, in gangs, and even for use against themselves in acts of suicide (mainly in Northern countries). According to the World Health Organisation, males are three to six times more likely than females to commit murder, with most victims and assailants drawn from the ranks of men aged 18–49.[37] However, women's roles as users and supporters of the proliferation and misuse of arms should not be overlooked.

Box 6: Women in the Maoist insurgency in Nepal

Women are visible at all levels of the People's War in Nepal. Every third Maoist guerrilla and every tenth combatant is a woman. Women have become area commanders, and some of the most violent actions are associated with all-women guerrilla squads armed with *Khrukris* and sawn-off muskets, although 303 rifles, AK-47s, and farm implements are also used by the guerrillas. The female combatants are trained in the use of these small arms, while others work in transportation, communications, and intelligence as spies, couriers, and messengers, thus promoting their proliferation and misuse.[38]

Despite the limited availability of statistics differentiated by age and gender, one can perceive some generalised gender-based patterns in a study of the impact of small arms. In many cultures, guns symbolise male power. Guns therefore have come to represent both power and security for many men. Men are at greatest risk of small-arms injury or death as combatants in conflict. Sixty-five per cent of all patients wounded in war and admitted to Red Cross hospitals in Afghanistan, Rwanda, Chechnya, and the border regions of Kenya and Cambodia between 1991 and 1998 were male, aged between 16 and 50 years.[39]

For some women, the possession of arms may be an expression of empowerment or liberation in a male-orientated culture. For others, small arms may be viewed as a threat to themselves and their families, either as victims of weapons in the household, or as mothers and carers. In conflict, women and girls are at greatest risk of small-arms injury or death as civilians. They are targets of rape and sexual violence, including sexual torture, forced prostitution (in the role of combatants' 'wives'), and forced impregnation and HIV transmission, often at the point of a gun. Women are strategic targets in conflict because of their role as biological, cultural, and social reproducers of society. Women and girls are targets of trafficking for prostitution via physical or economic coercion. In more stable times, women and girls are at greatest risk from harm in their own homes as victims of domestic violence, often at gun-point.

Box 7: Rape as a weapon of war in the Democratic Republic of Congo

'Sexual violence has been used as a weapon of war by most of the forces involved in the conflict ... Some rapists aggravated their crimes by other acts of extraordinary brutality, shooting victims in the vagina or mutilating them with knives or razor blades. Some attacked girls as young as five years of age or elderly women as old as eighty.'[40]

Box 8: Domestic violence in Cambodia

'Approximately a quarter of victims' husbands owned guns, and these were most often used to "threaten or coerce women"'. Eighteen per cent of the battered women were threatened with a gun, four per cent with a grenade or bayonet.'[41]

Women and girls may experience a great sense of social and economic alienation as a result of a small-arms injury. A woman or girl rejected by her husband or family because she has been raped or maimed by a weapon will, for example, suffer from the social stigma of her attack and find it more difficult to support herself or her children economically. Women and girls represent the majority of health providers and 'carers' dealing with victims of armed conflict and gun crime.

In the absence of men who are fighting or killed, women carry the economic burden of sustaining families through daily household survival. For example, after the Rwandan genocide, it was estimated that 70 per cent of the population was female and that 50 per cent of all households were headed by women.[42]

Understanding what motivates men and women to misuse small arms can help to establish an understanding of what creates the demand for them in the first place, and thus how to respond to the problem at local, national, regional, and international levels. For example, understanding why men or women take up arms will influence what incentives are provided – for men and for women – in any disarmament programme.

Understanding the differing gender-based impacts of small arms will also help to develop responses that reflect the needs of the whole community (men, women, boys, and girls). For example, there is a need to design services to respond to the physical injury, the social alienation, the economic poverty, and the psychological trauma of victims and perpetrators of small-arms violence, reflecting the differences in how men and women are affected by small arms and how they can be reintegrated into society.

The impact of small arms on development

The widespread availability of SALW can have serious negative consequences for development in a variety of contexts. Whether societies are suffering conflict, emerging from conflict, or enjoying relative peace and stability, the availability and use of SALW can block, undermine, and erode efforts to achieve sustainable development.

Although it is widely recognised that SALW do not, in themselves, cause conflicts, they can make recourse to violence more likely, while at the same time prolonging and increasing the lethality of that violence.[43] Possibilities for development are generally extremely limited in an environment characterised by extreme instability or SALW-related violence. This is particularly the case in rural communities, often among the poorest and most insecure. Vulnerable to armed groups from outside or within their midst, they often feel that they have no choice but to take up arms in self-defence. One inevitable result is reduced agricultural production and increased poverty. In East Africa, for example, an increased level of armed violence among pastoralist communities has had a serious negative impact on development: traditional and State governance systems have been undermined, and efforts to reduce the marginalisation of these communities have been frustrated.[44] Development in urban communities too can be imperilled by violence and conflict. For example, armed sectarian conflict in Karachi has resulted in reduced capital investment and the relocation of employment opportunities, thereby contributing to a cycle of poverty and further violence.[45]

In post-conflict situations, if SALW are not speedily removed from former combatants and from society as a whole, people may continue to rely on them for economic gain and personal security. This may perpetuate high levels of SALW-related casualties and an associated climate of fear and instability within which it is extremely difficult for sustainable development to take place. In Cambodia and Afghanistan, casualty and injury rates among civilians remained high, despite the conclusion of peace agreements, with the annual incidence of weapons injuries in parts of Afghanistan declining by only 30 to 40 per cent in the 1995-97 period, compared with the incidence at the height of the conflict between 1991 and 1995.[46]

Even in countries where there is no recent experience of armed conflict, widespread availability and use of SALW can take their toll on society, with the economic costs of injury and death from violent gun crime threatening to compromise development goals. In countries such as South Africa, Colombia, Brazil, and Jamaica, where there are very high homicide rates, up to 98 per cent of murders have involved the use of firearms.[47]

In all of the above situations, high levels of deaths and injuries from SALW impose great economic and social burdens, undermining social infrastructure, including the provision of health care. In developing countries these resources are often, at the same time, limited in extent and vastly over-burdened; hence, where there are large numbers of SALW casualties, scarce resources may be stretched to breaking point.

Besides the immediate consequences of high SALW-related casualty rates, sustainable development in societies suffering from high levels of SALW violence may be undermined at a more fundamental level. Reduced economic activity on the part of the victims of SALW-related violence, and on the part of those family members who may be charged with caring for the injured and maimed, can have serious repercussions. For example, detailed studies in the USA estimate costs from premature death and injury due to firearms at some $100 billion per year,[48] while the Inter-American Development Bank has calculated the regional economic costs of armed violence to be some $144–170 billion per year during the late 1990s.[49]

It is clear that the proliferation and misuse of SALW can frustrate efforts at sustainable development in urban and rural communities of North and South. Accordingly, tackling the SALW problem is a prerequisite if concerted progress is to be made towards fulfilling the Millennium Development Goals outlined in the United Nations Millennium Declaration in September 2000.

3 Recommended measures to address the proliferation and misuse of small arms and light weapons

In view of the many harmful effects of the proliferation and misuse of SALW, the following section introduces a range of measures to address the demand for weapons and to better regulate their supply.

It may be the case that your decision to take action on small-arms issues is based either on the impact of SALW on your community or on the role of the country in which you are based in the supply of SALW. The 'demand' element of this section may be of greatest relevance to you if you are motivated to tackle the incidence of violent gun crime in your community. In this regard, tackling the demand for small arms covers a broad range of issues, including structural and deep-rooted problems such as poverty, inequality, bad governance, and underdevelopment, in addition to more specific initiatives to tackle the weapons themselves, such as regulating the activities of private military and security companies, reforming the security sector, managing stockpiles of weapons, destroying stocks of surplus weapons, and transforming cultures of violence.

On the other hand, if you are seeking to take action to encourage tougher regulation of the SALW trade, then the 'supply' element of this section will be most relevant. It covers action to regulate the production and transfer of SALW, including the establishment of effective controls on weapons transfers; monitoring the end-use of small arms once exported or transferred; the establishment of systems for marking and tracing individual weapons; the regulation of arms brokering and shipping agents; establishment of controls on the production of SALW overseas; and instituting stringent controls on the possession and use of SALW by civilians.

For a fully effective response to the problem of SALW proliferation, action in both areas is crucial. Where possible and appropriate, it will be important to link your action with that of others working on different aspects of the problem, so that a comprehensive approach is maintained. To find out more about the wide variety of actions being undertaken by civil society on the various aspects of the small-arms problem, contact the International Action Network on Small Arms (IANSA) – details in Part 4 of this handbook.

Measures to address the demand for SALW

Reducing the demand for arms in affected communities requires an understanding of why communities or individuals resort to arms in the first place. A complex web of social, cultural, political, and economic conditions determines the demand, and thus it is necessary to take a holistic view of the situation, which will probably involve addressing fundamental issues of poverty and impunity. Reform of the policing and criminal-justice systems may be necessary, but alternatives to using guns to create livelihoods must also be considered.

There must also be genuine, active engagement of the local community to ensure that any initiatives are relevant to their needs. Men, women, girls, boys, older people, disabled people, and members of all ethnic and religious groups should be consulted and should feel a sense of ownership of any resulting plan. Ex-combatants and ex-gang members from different sides may have much in common with each other and can act powerfully for change in challenging machismo and gun culture. Elders' voices are often critical; for youth, alternatives must be found to provide the sense of identity, purpose, group support, and security that membership of gangs can offer.

Weapons collection

It is widely recognised that the removal of weapons from society is an important means of reducing the proliferation and misuse of SALW. In recent years, weapons-collection initiatives have been undertaken around the world when a country or a community wishes to put an end to a violent or traumatic period in its history. In this regard, as well as helping to reduce numbers of SALW circulating in society, weapons-collection initiatives may also serve as potent symbols of hope for a more peaceful future.

Weapons-collection initiatives may be divided into two broad categories. Some relate to crime-prevention programmes: for example, the amnesty organised by the UK government in March 1996 following the massacre of 16 primary-school children and their teacher in Dunblane, Scotland: in this instance, 185,000 SALW were surrendered. A similar initiative was undertaken by the Australian government following the killing of 35 people at Port Arthur, Tasmania in April 1996; this initiative resulted in the surrender of 644,000 weapons.[50] Some NGOs such as the Brazil-based Viva Rio are becoming a driving force behind such initiatives within a crime-prevention context.

Weapons-collection initiatives have also been undertaken within the context of post-conflict reconstruction and peace-building programmes. Where violent conflict has recently abated, efforts to remove weapons from society must be coupled with initiatives to address the root causes of conflict, as in the cases of

Sierra Leone and Northern Ireland.[51] Failure to take a comprehensive approach to post-conflict reconstruction and peace-building can mean that demand for SALW remains, thereby undermining efforts to remove these weapons from society as a whole.

An essential feature of any effort to resolve conflict and build a stable peace must be the speedy and effective demobilisation and reintegration of former combatants when hostilities have ceased. Experience with demobilisation and reintegration programmes (DRPs) conducted after peace agreements in the late 1980s and early 1990s (as in Nicaragua, El Salvador, Mozambique, and Liberia) demonstrated the problems that arise from inadequate provisions for SALW collection and control from former combatants.[52] For example, groups of ex-combatants who retain easy access to arms may resort to banditry in the absence of alternative sources of income, or continued insurrection in the absence of a viable peace agreement. Accordingly, the instigation of DRPs which incorporate provisions for swift collection of SALW, accurate record-keeping, safe storage of collected SALW, and their speedy destruction can help to ensure that peace, once established, is maintained.

Where excess weapons in society are linked to conflicts which have long since ended, as in El Salvador and Cambodia, weapons-collection initiatives take on a different character. Under these circumstances, holders of weapons may be reluctant to relinquish them, if they have grown to rely on them as part of their daily life. Accordingly it will be necessary to employ a range of measures, possibly including the use of incentives or rewards for individuals who surrender SALW, and efforts to assure the safety of the civil population.

In recent years, weapons-collection initiatives have been undertaken in Albania, Australia, Brazil, Cambodia, El Salvador, Georgia, Liberia, Macedonia, Mali, Mozambique, Sierra Leone, South Africa, and the UK, to name but a few countries. One of the most high-profile initiatives, due to its pioneering use of the concept of 'disarmament for development', has been the Gramsch Project in Albania. This project linked the provision of assistance for building social infrastructure such as roads and schools to the surrender of weapons by the local community. The pilot phase of the Gramsch project, from early 1999 until 2000, led to the surrender of 6000 weapons and 137 tons of ammunition in exchange for assistance worth US $1.2 million.[53] Although relatively costly, the Gramsch project is widely seen as a success because of the awareness-raising value of the project, and the permanent benefits arising from the rewards.[54]

Recommendations for best practice in weapons-collection programmes

Governments, together with civil-society organisations, should seek to set up weapons-collection programmes whenever there is an opportunity to do so.

Information-exchange and capacity-building programmes, including technical and financial assistance, should also be undertaken, in order to promote an international understanding of best practice. Generally speaking, sustainable weapons-collection initiatives are characterised as follows:

- They are coupled with efforts to tackle the root causes of conflicts and to promote respect for human rights and fundamental freedoms.
- They benefit from the active support of all protagonists, thus ensuring that all parties concerned have the confidence to relinquish arms.
- There is wider public support for the initiative.
- They are accompanied by measures to control access to SALW on the part of civilians.
- An appropriate balance is struck between the imposition of sanctions and the provision of incentives.
- All weapons seized and surrendered are quickly destroyed, to prevent their re-circulation into society.

Reform of the security sector

The police and the military are usually responsible for maintaining law and order in times of peace. However, security forces may themselves be responsible for the proliferation and misuse of small arms, especially if they are repressive, corrupt, and unaccountable, and if the judicial system is unable to take effective action to prosecute the perpetrators and enforce legislation.

The absence of a viable security sector results in the privatisation of security, which can ultimately fuel demand and lead to an increase in civilian possession of SALW. In a situation where the security sector is an active agent of insecurity, weapons may be sought by citizens to defend themselves against the State, and an inefficient or corrupt security sector will not be able to properly monitor or regulate the private possession or use of firearms.

Under such circumstances, Security Sector Reform (SSR) Programmes may be useful in preventing the proliferation of SALW at the national level. The overall aim of Security Sector Reform is the transformation of the security sector (police, military, judicial bodies, etc.) so that they play an effective, legitimate, and democratically accountable role in providing external and internal security for citizens. The ultimate aim should be the provision of a reasonable and acceptable level of security to the whole of society, regardless of social or financial status.

Recommendations for best practice in Security Sector Reform Programmes

- Strengthening civilian control and oversight of the security sector, which may include the 'civilianisation' of ministries of defence and the interior; promoting independent, non-government expertise on security-sector issues; and the development of greater transparency and trust between civilian and military institutions.

- Increasing professionalism within the security forces and enhancing the capacity of the armed forces to monitor and regulate firearms use, by means of technical skills training; the upgrading of military or police equipment; better remuneration for personnel; and strengthening police capacity to guarantee a basic level of human security.
- Establishing Disarmament, Demobilisation, and Reintegration (DDR) programmes, under which regular and irregular forces have their arms taken into public control, and any weapons that are surplus to the needs of any new security forces are destroyed.
- Strengthening the rule of law and establishing strong independent legal frameworks, by means of law reform and capacity building for both judiciaries and parliamentarians, to make the system more responsive to the needs of the general public; and establishing an independent judiciary to counter the need for people to seek justice through informal mechanisms.

Box 9: The case for security-sector reform: Brazil

'The systematic use of torture and ill-treatment continued in police stations, prisons and juvenile detention centres. Killings by police and "death squads" linked to the security forces increased, especially in urban centres. Land reform activists and indigenous people involved in land disputes were harassed, assaulted and killed both by military police and by gunmen hired by local landowners, with the apparent acquiescence of the police and the authorities. Elizabeth Cristina de Oliveira Maia was shot dead outside her home on 26 September [2000], just before giving evidence at the appeal hearing of one of the military police accused of involvement in the Candelária massacre. Her murder suggested the involvement of a "death squad", and increased the fears of other witnesses in "death squad" trials.

João Elizio Lima Pessoa was driving to his home in Aguas Lindas, Goiás state, on 7 February. The road was blocked by rocks and when he tried to clear them he was shot dead. His wife was also shot, but survived. João Elizio Lima Pessoa had been working with the Public Security Community Council, investigating "death squad" killings in the region.'[55]

Private military and security companies and the proliferation and misuse of small arms

During the 1990s a change occurred in the nature of conflicts, as the volume of available weaponry increased, and the types of actor engaged in violence multiplied. A feature of this change has been the continuing, if not growing, presence of mercenaries (individuals who fight for financial gain in foreign conflicts) and the emergence of private companies contracted to provide military and security services. These services range from logistical support and training to procurement of arms and on-the-ground involvement in fighting. There are a number of specific ways in which mercenaries and private military and security companies can fuel the proliferation and misuse of small arms. They include the following:

- acting as arms brokers and transportation agents;
- violating UN arms embargoes;
- carrying out human-rights abuses and breaches of international humanitarian law, or facilitating such violations through training or equipping abusive forces;
- driving the demand for small arms in communities by contributing to the militarisation of societies and the exacerbation of tensions in the regions in which they operate.

To date, action to control mercenaries and private military and security companies has been sporadic and *ad hoc* – with serious consequences for peace, security, and human rights. In order to reduce the proliferation and misuse of SALW that have resulted from a growth in the privatisation of security, all States should consider taking the following measures.

Recommendations for the control of private military and security companies

- Introduce national legislation to control the activities of private military and security companies. The latter should be required to register and apply for authorisation for each contract which they sign. Such applications must be assessed in accordance with publicly available criteria, based on international human-rights standards and international humanitarian law.
- Ban mercenary activity, by ratifying the International Convention against the Recruitment, Use, Financing and Training of Mercenaries, to ensure that the convention enters into force. It is necessary to negotiate a protocol to this treaty, to ensure that the activities of private military and security companies are regulated internationally.

Management of stockpiles and surplus SALW

Vast quantities of SALW – including semi-automatic and military-style equipment – are held by armed forces, police, and other State bodies. These stocks are a prime target for criminals, bandits, and armed groups. Losses from State stocks through theft, corruption, or neglect represent a major source of illicit weapons. These losses may take place with the knowledge or collusion of those in possession of, or responsible for managing, State-owned firearms; they may also occur without the detailed knowledge of the State and its agencies – particularly where accounting systems and procedures for stockpile management are inadequate.

The security of arms stockpiles is a particular problem in regions suffering conflict or serious political and social upheaval. For example, rebel army groups and bandits in Liberia, Sierra Leone, Ethiopia, Congo Republic, and the Transcaucasus have obtained arms and ammunition by seizing stocks from police and army units or stores.[56] The example of Albania has also been well documented: well over 650,000 SALW were looted from State arsenals there during the turmoil of 1997. At the same time, many developing countries and those in political or economic transition, such as many of the former Soviet Republics, maintain large holdings of SALW but lack the resources or systems to prevent losses through theft, corruption, or neglect.[57]

Compounding the problems associated with stockpile management in many countries is the issue of surplus weapons, i.e. those held by armed forces, police, and other State agencies that are surplus to their requirements. The surplus may have been caused by a restructuring or re-equipment process or the implementation of a post-conflict peace accord.[58] Until recently, countries have typically taken less care when transferring surplus weapons than when exporting newly manufactured weapons, rendering it more likely that such weapons will enter the 'grey' or illicit market.

Ensuring proper management of and accountability for State-owned stocks of SALW in all countries is a major challenge, requiring significant organisational and financial resources. If it could be achieved, however, it would make a significant contribution towards reducing the level of the illicit trade in and use of SALW globally.

Recommendations for the management of stockpiles and surplus weaponry

- All authorities should take full responsibility for all weapons held or issued by them and ensure that they are protected against theft, corruption, or neglect. States should begin by reviewing and assessing the adequacy of current procedures and practices and should repeat this process on a regular basis.

- States should ensure that they have adequate systems and procedures in place relating to appropriate locations for SALW stockpiles; physical security measures; control of access to stocks; inventory management and accounting control; staff training; security of transport for SALW; security and accounting procedures for SALW held by operational units; methods for detecting losses and levying sanctions against those responsible.[59]
- States should ensure that all surplus weapons, parts, components, and ammunition are destroyed and not re-exported.
- The UN and other international and regional organisations should promote and ensure stockpile security, particularly where involved in peace-keeping operations. International awareness-raising and capacity-building programmes should be established in order to develop common understandings of best practice and to assist countries that lack resources and expertise in the implementation of the same.

Measures to control the supply and transfer of SALW

A prerequisite for effective international action to combat the proliferation and misuse of small arms and light weapons is that States should develop a common understanding of what constitutes the 'legal' trade and therefore of what is 'illicit' (see the 'Definitions' section earlier in this handbook). Failure to exert effective control over the legal trade in SALW opens up possibilities for diversion to illicit markets and end-users, and blurs the lines between the legal and illicit trades. In some circumstances inadequate controls on the 'State-authorised' trade in SALW also result in weapons flowing directly to abusive end-users.

All governments are potential suppliers of SALW, since even those with no manufacturing capacity have the potential to export surplus or confiscated weapons from the stocks maintained by the police and/or armed forces. The nature of the export, import, in-transit licensing, and end-use certification requirements imposed by governments, and the rigour (or lack of rigour) with which they are monitored and enforced, are therefore of great international importance. Governments have a significant role to play in ensuring that transfers of SALW are not authorised to abusive end-users or diverted to illicit markets.

A few basic questions immediately present themselves. What are the circumstances under which States ought (or ought not) to authorise a transfer of small arms and light weapons? How are these decisions to be made? What sorts of factor ought States to take into account when making these decisions?

The first and most obvious answer to these questions is that, at the very least, States ought not to authorise transfers of SALW that would violate their commitments under national and international law. This basic obligation, widely accepted by the international community, is reflected by the UN Disarmament Commission, which defines the illicit trade in SALW as

> *that international trade in conventional arms, which is contrary to the laws of States and/or international law.*[60]

It is also reflected in the UN Programme of Action to Prevent, Combat, and Eradicate the Illicit Trade in Small Arms and Light Weapons in All its Aspects (PoA), which recognised the importance of exercising effective control over SALW according to the established standards of international law. Section II, Article 11 of the PoA reads partly as follows:

> *Member States undertake to... assess applications for export authorisations according to strict national regulations and procedures that cover all small arms and light weapons and are consistent with the existing responsibilities of States under relevant international law.*[61]

Therefore it is clear that the existing responsibilities of States under relevant international law represent a critical set of norms for decision making in this area. They are the fundamentals of any effective SALW transfer-control system.

What, then, are these international responsibilities? And how can States develop transfer-control regimes that are consistent with them?

Some of the prohibitions that are established by international law in this area are relatively clear and uncontroversial; these are called *express prohibitions.*

Express prohibitions

The most basic form of prohibition is a multilateral (between several States) or bilateral (between two States) agreement to ban transfers. With the exception of anti-personnel mines, the only specific agreement completely prohibiting transfers of small arms and light weapons currently in force is the regional and non-binding three-year moratorium concluded by ECOWAS in 1998 and subsequently extended for a further three-year period in 2001.

Other prohibitions on transfers to specific countries or recipients include arms embargoes and other sanctions imposed by the United Nations Security Council. Such decisions to impose arms embargoes are taken under Chapter VII of the UN Charter and thus are binding on all members of the UN. Obligations exist on two levels: first, States themselves are prohibited from transferring the weapons to the embargoed State; and secondly, they must also take the necessary measures to implement, apply, and enforce the embargo internally, to make it effective against private actors within their jurisdiction. In March 2003, there were UN embargoes in place against Iraq, Liberia, Libya, Rwanda, and Sierra Leone. In addition to these UN-mandated embargoes, which are legally binding, some regional organisations also impose arms embargoes on a particular State or armed group, and these should be equally respected by Member States when taking decisions about the control of SALW exports. For instance, during the conflict in East Timor in 1999, the European Union imposed an embargo on weapons transfers to Indonesia.

Restrictions based on use

Another relevant type of prohibition derived from international law is based on the use to which the weapons will be put. This type of prohibition has not gained the same level of acceptance among States as the preceding categories of restriction. It would apply to circumstances where a State transferring weapons had knowledge, or ought to have had knowledge, that the arms in question were likely to be used for serious violations of international law by the recipients. This prohibition is based on the well-established international legal principle that States must refrain from providing aid or assistance to other States in the commission of internationally classified wrongful acts.

The principle is stated in Article 16 of the International Law Commission's Articles on Responsibility of States for Internationally Wrongful Acts, adopted in 2001, in the following terms:

> *A State which aids or assists another State in the commission of an internationally wrongful act by the latter is internationally responsible for doing so if:*
>
> *that State does so with knowledge of the circumstances of the internationally wrongful act; and*
> *the act would be internationally wrongful if committed by that State.*

The kinds of internationally wrongful act that would be covered by such a prohibition include the following:

- breaches of the United Nations Charter or corresponding rules of customary international law, in particular those prohibiting the threat or use of force in international relations
- serious violations of human rights
- serious violations of international humanitarian law relating to international or non-international armed conflict
- genocide or crimes against humanity
- acts of terrorism.

Areas of emerging international consensus and best practice

Beyond the restrictions that reflect States' commitments under international law, there are a number of other factors that governments, to a greater or lesser extent, take into account when deciding whether to grant or refuse an export licence for SALW. These include:

- the threat of use of SALW in conflict
- the potential effect on international/regional stability
- the undermining of sustainable development
- the risk of diversion or trans-shipment to an illicit end-user.

There have been attempts over recent years in some countries (for instance, South Africa) and groups of countries (for instance, the EU and OSCE) to codify some of their commitments under international law. These efforts are not comprehensive; however, they are important in that they provide useful benchmarks for the future.

Box 10: The Arms Trade Treaty

A group of non-government organisations (NGOs)[62] partnered by international lawyers are advocating the establishment of an 'Arms Trade Treaty' or 'ATT'. Drawing on existing international law, the ATT is a model for a legally binding international agreement establishing a set of minimum standards and procedures for the transfer of conventional weapons, including SALW.[63] It is based on the simple principle that arms exporters have a responsibility to ensure that they do not provide weapons that would be used in serious violations of international law. To date, this effort has been endorsed by 18 individuals and organisations honoured with the Nobel Peace Prize.[64]

The ATT establishes core, common minimum standards for international arms transfers, and a workable mechanism for the application of these standards. Under this instrument, a transfer would not be authorised if there was a risk that the arms might be used to violate human rights and international humanitarian law or to commit war crimes, genocide, or crimes against humanity. Furthermore, there would be a presumption of denial on arms transfers which were likely to undermine sustainable development, political stability, or regional security, or to facilitate the commission of violent crimes. Under this treaty, States would submit an annual report to an international registry on all the international arms transfers from or through its territory or subject to its authorisation. The registry would subsequently publish an annual report of these State-sanctioned transfers.

Establishing effective operative procedures

Truly effective controls on the transfer and end-use of SALW must begin with comprehensive and stringently enforced national controls and procedures. However, national procedures are not sufficient in themselves. Because of the transnational nature of the production and export of SALW, regional and international controls are also required.

In recent years States have recognised the necessity for transnational controls. For example, in 1997 the Inter-American Convention and subsequent development of Model Regulations for the Control of the International Movement of Firearms developed a control framework for export, import, and transit licensing and authorisation in the Americas region. Some elements of this Convention have been subsequently internationalised by the UN Firearms Protocol against the Illicit Manufacturing and Trafficking in Firearms, Their Parts and Components and Ammunition (see Section 4 of Part 1 of this book).

If an international small-arms control system is to prove effective, it is vital that common standards for licensing transfers are established. In order to ensure that shipments of SALW are not diverted to unauthorised end-users or used for other illegal or undesirable purposes, States should consider implementing the following initiatives.

Recommendations for establishing effective licensing controls and procedures

- All transfers of SALW should be explicitly authorised by the exporting, importing, and transit States involved in any transfer.
- All States involved in any transfer should exchange information, such as detailed descriptions of the goods being shipped, including quantities, the final destination of the arms, and the identity of the end-user. Information should also be exchanged about the dispatch and/or receipt of the shipments of SALW.
- No exports should be made without receipt by the exporting authority of the necessary certification from the importing and transit States. Similarly, authorities in transit States should require receipt of official export and import authorisations before allowing onward shipment.
- Provision should be made for exporting States to verify the delivery of SALW, including physical inspection within the importing State (see below).

End-use certification and monitoring

End-use certification and monitoring procedures are vital for the credibility of export-control systems. Without them governments, parliaments, and the public cannot be sure that the SALW transfers that governments have authorised in accordance with national export criteria are not being misused by the end-user or have not been diverted to illegitimate recipients. Current procedures for establishing and monitoring the end-use of SALW transferred from many major exporting States are inadequate.

False end-use documentation is often used to divert arms – particularly small arms – to the illicit market. For example, UN bodies set up to assess compliance with sanctions against UNITA forces in Angola found that large quantities of weapons had been exported from Bulgaria to the Angolan rebel movement on the basis of forged end-use certificates and assurances.[65] Since formats and procedures vary greatly from country to country, end-use assurances and certification are especially liable to abuse and fraud. Forged statements are used to gain export licences for weapons that were never intended for their stated destination or purpose. As few countries physically verify delivery, forgery is a low-risk strategy.

There have been numerous cases brought to light, primarily by civil-society researchers and journalists, of the consequences of poor end-use controls and the lack of follow up monitoring.

Box 11: Finnish bullets

During a May 1999 research mission to Indonesia and East Timor, Amnesty International collected the casings of SALW bullets, found after a paramilitary militia attack in the Dili area of East Timor. These bullet casings were later analysed and found to have been manufactured by the Finnish company Patria Lapua Oy. The Finnish government has in the past admitted granting export licences for ammunition to the Indonesian security forces. But how did such ammunition fall into the hands of paramilitary groups?

Recommendations for developing effective end-use and monitoring procedures

- The most effective system for end-use control would include provisions whereby an end-use certificate takes the form of a legally binding contract, which contains a list of proscribed uses (such as human-rights abuses) and a prohibition on unauthorised re-export or transfer.
- Failure to honour the terms of an end-use contract should result in the revocation of the licence and a halt in further supplies, provision of spares, maintenance, and training.
- A comprehensive system of follow-up checks is also required and should be provided for within the contract to ensure that exported goods are not misused by their stated end-user, or are not being diverted, or re-exported. The requisite checks could be carried out by consular or embassy officials based in the country of destination.

Regulating civilian ownership of SALW

Civilian-owned SALW have contributed to violence, death, and injuries throughout the world. It is estimated that around the world there are as many small arms in civilian possession as there are under State control.[66] Accordingly, the strict regulation of domestic SALW ownership is a crucial aspect of efforts to tackle the illicit trade in, and use of, these weapons.

Most SALW are legally manufactured and acquired by governments or civilians. Some SALW are manufactured illegally and enter civilian hands without proper authorisation of the State. However, this problem is largely confined to particular regions of the world – such as Central America or South Asia. Other SALW are illegally imported into a country under cover of false documentation, such as customs declarations. Some SALW are legally acquired and then modified to the point where they are no longer legal under the laws of a particular country: for example, the conversion of a semi-automatic weapon to a fully automatic one. Other SALW in civilian possession are illegally sold on by the original legal owner, while hundreds of thousands of civilian-owned SALW are stolen every year.[67] Finally, weapons surrendered by the public in gun amnesties can also find their way into illegal civil possession if they are not properly safeguarded and destroyed.

Many regional and international agreements[68] have referred to the need for strict domestic regulation of SALW possession and use – including adequate control, marking, record-keeping, transparency in relation to the level and purposes of civilian SALW ownership, and proper enforcement of legislation. For example, co-operative arrangements have been established through a Protocol to the UN Convention on Transnational Organised Crime (the so-called Firearms Protocol), requiring countries to provide authorisation to one another before allowing commercial shipments of firearms to enter or move across their territory. The UN Firearms Protocol also establishes minimum standards for marking of small arms, and it is hoped that together these measures will help to prevent the diversion of SALW from legal civilian ownership into illicit markets.

Despite the increasing international attention given to the issue, the stringency of regulations governing civilian ownership of SALW varies significantly from country to country. Some States, such as the UK, allow only very limited categories of SALW to be owned by civilians; others, such as the USA, allow civilian ownership of even military-style assault rifles.

Recommendations for best practice in the control of civilian possession of SALW

In order to reduce opportunities for the diversion of civilian-owned weapons to illicit end-users, all countries need to adopt comparable stringent regulations governing the domestic ownership and use of SALW. These measures should include:

- Prohibiting the civilian ownership of certain categories of SALW, particularly military-style weapons and hand-guns.
- Regulating SALW dealers and ensuring that they are required to meet adequate standards of record-keeping.
- Maintaining strict licensing requirements so that individuals may not own and use SALW unless they have obtained express authorisation from the appropriate State body. Securing this authorisation should require demonstration of legitimate 'need' as well as rigorous checks on the authenticity of the application and the character of the applicant.

- Ensuring high standards of marking and record-keeping for civilian-owned SALW.
- Imposing strict requirements for safe storage of civilian-owned SALW.

Reporting, transparency, and accountability (including parliamentary reporting)

Efforts to combat and prevent illicit trafficking in, and proliferation and misuse of, small arms and light weapons are hampered by lack of publicly available information. Official information concerning the production, stockpiling, and transfer of SALW is either non-existent or generally shrouded in excessive secrecy. Such secrecy undermines systems of accountability within each country. It also obstructs inter-agency co-ordination and appropriate international co-operation. Many governments do not collect, maintain, or exchange sufficient information even for their national control purposes.

Currently at least 60 States are regularly involved in the legal export of SALW, while almost all countries in the world are involved in the legal import of SALW and occasional export of surplus second-hand weapons. About 30 countries provide public information on their annual arms transfers, normally in the form of a report to parliament. However, only three States (USA, Italy, and UK) provide systematic public information on both the value and volume of their transfers of SALW by country destination.

In addition to national export reports, at least 33 countries currently provide information on both imports and exports of SALW to the COMTRADE database – an international customs database administered by the UN Statistical Division. However, a number of the world's major exporters of SALW, including Bulgaria, Israel, and the Russian Federation, do not submit data to COMTRADE.

Recommendations for enhancing transparency and accountability

- Governments should review current present arrangements for disclosing information relating to SALW and to the implementation of the UN PoA and other regional agreements.
- Governments should undertake to implement existing voluntary commitments on transparency and accountability at the national, regional, and global levels.
- All producing and exporting governments should publish annual reports on arms production, export licences, and transfers; the reports should include information relating to quantities, values, and end-users.
- There should be opportunities for parliaments in exporting States to examine applications and advise government prior to their being granted or refused.

Marking and tracing

The marking and tracing of small arms has attracted considerable attention and interest in recent years. Firearms and ammunition can be marked with simple inscriptions to show the type of item, serial number, manufacturer, and initial purchaser. These elements allow the firearm to be registered and subsequently identified. The process of reconstituting the transfer route that is followed by a specific weapon over the course of its lifetime is known as 'tracing'. Successful tracing, dependent on adequate marking and record keeping, allows concerned governments and organisations to identify the producer of a particular weapon and the various intermediaries involved in its transfer to, for example, human-rights abusers, criminal groups, or to conflict zones. Tracing will also enable illicit trafficking networks to be uncovered and destroyed, and for actors involved in the deliberate violation of international arms embargoes to be punished – in theory. In practice, existing marking, record keeping and tracing arrangements are on the whole inadequate to the task.

Recommendations for enhancing marking and tracing

- The current UN process on marking and tracing needs to move towards the negotiation of an international, legally binding instrument on marking and tracing of SALW.
- To promote implementation and development of the commitments contained in the UN PoA, a system of information exchange on national marking systems (including country-identification marks) needs to be established.
- An international programme is needed to identify and disseminate good practices relating to marking, record-keeping and tracing; to establish guidelines and minimum standards for marking each type of SALW (including ammunition); and to assess and promote reliable marking techniques.
- As well as controlling direct transfers from one State to another, States must also close other loopholes which facilitate illicit trafficking. Two important ones are Brokering and Licensed Production Overseas (LPO).

Brokering and shipping agents

Arms brokers may be defined as middlemen who organise arms transfers between two or more parties, often bringing together buyers, sellers, transporters, financiers, and insurers to make a deal. They generally do so for financial gain, although political or religious motivation may also play a part in some deals. Often such brokers do not reside in the country from which the weapons originate, nor do they live in the country through which the weapons pass, or the one for which they are destined. As a result, such 'third party' arms brokering is notoriously difficult to trace, monitor, or control. Arms brokers work very closely with transport or shipping agents. These agents contract transport facilities, carriers, and crews in order to move arms cargoes by sea, air, rail, or road.

Evidence suggests that many of the arms transfers to the worst-affected conflict regions and human-rights crisis zones are organised and trafficked by arms brokering and transport agents. Targeting those States with weak national export controls and enforcement, unscrupulous brokers and transportation agents organise the transfer of arms and security equipment to a range of illegitimate end-users such as criminals, terrorists, and human-rights abusers.

Box 12: Brokers breach embargoes

European arms brokers and transport agents have been implicated in the breaching of a number of UN arms embargoes. One example is the role they played in circumventing the embargo in place against the Revolutionary United Front in Sierra Leone. The RUF had been responsible for widespread and gross abuses of human rights, including mass killings, rape, torture, and amputation.

On 13 March 1999 a shipment of 68 tons of Ukrainian arms was flown to Ouagadougou, Burkina Faso. The shipment, organised by a Gibraltar company, contained more than 700 boxes of weapons and cartridges. It was flown in an Antonov aircraft run by a UK company, Air Foyle. The weapons were subsequently trans-shipped to Liberia. From there such arms could then be easily shipped across the border to the RUF forces, waiting eagerly.[69]

Recommendations for controlling arms brokers

- Governments need to introduce national measures to control brokering. These should apply to the buying, selling, and promotion of SALW. All such brokering transactions should require the licensed approval of government and be judged on the same strict export criteria as direct SALW transfers (see above).
- To be effective, such controls must apply to all nationals, wherever they live, and to any company or individual resident or registered in the country. Such measures would help to ensure that brokers are unable to escape regulation simply by stepping outside the country.
- In addition, governments should require nationals who are arms brokers to register as such and to publish their audited accounts relating to arms trading. Agents who break laws regulating SALW exports or deliberately

supply misleading information about their SALW transactions should be prosecuted and banned from any further arms brokering.

- Governments should also work towards internationalising controls on arms brokering, to ensure that arms brokers and trafficking agents do not simply relocate from States where regulations are in place to States where control is lacking.

Licensed production overseas

Licensed production overseas (LPO) is the practice by which one company allows and enables a second company in another country to manufacture its products under licence. Under such agreements, the licensee may receive a range of support from the licensing company in the form of component parts, machine tools, blue prints, and technical drawings; technical personnel such as engineers may be seconded to work on the project. LPO and the associated transfer of SALW production technology mean that new companies and countries can now initiate SALW production where none had previously taken place. The proliferation of such LPO has not been matched by the parallel development of effective controls. The effects of such poor control can be deadly.

Box 13: Heckler and Koch

The Anglo-German company Heckler and Koch has engaged in a number of LPO arrangements with the State-owned Turkish arms manufacturer MKEK. In 1998, for example, Heckler and Koch won a ten-year contract worth US$ 18 million for the licensed production of 200,000 HK 5.56mm assault rifles in Turkey. While several States had previously refused direct arms supplies to Turkey in response to serious concerns about the abuse of human rights, this local production of H&K small arms allows the provisioning of the Turkish military and security forces.

Not only has licensed production allowed Turkey to equip its own police and military, but MKEK has also boosted its own export market and counts countries like Kuwait, Burundi, Libya, Pakistan, Tunisia, and Indonesia among its clients.

In a UK TV documentary programme broadcast on 9 December 1999, MKEK revealed that it had shipped a consignment of 500 MP5 submachine guns to the Indonesian police in August/September 1999. This was at a time when widespread violations of human rights were being committed in East Timor by anti-independence paramilitaries, allegedly with the complicity of the Indonesian security forces. On 16 September 1999, as the human-rights situation was deteriorating, the EU instituted a comprehensive arms embargo.

This embargo meant that neither Heckler and Koch in Germany nor the UK would have been allowed to export MP5s to Indonesia. However, since Turkey was not a member of the EU and was not covered by the embargo, little could be done to stop MKEK from producing H&K small arms under licence and from continuing to supply these weapons to the Indonesian security forces.

Recommendations for controlling Licensed Production Overseas

- States should not allow the transfer of licensed-production capability where there is a risk that the SALW subsequently produced will be transferred to an abusive end-user, or where the recipient State cannot demonstrate sufficient accountability in terms of end-use control.
- In those licensed production deals which are allowed, there must be strict control of production levels and the duration of the contract, and a prohibition on export without the originating government's consent.
- If there is evidence that the licensee has breached the contract and transferred products to those likely to use them for human-rights abuses or other proscribed purposes, then the licensed production agreement should be revoked. All provision of related machine tools, parts, training, and technology should then be halted.

4 Existing initiatives to address proliferation and misuse of SALW

This section considers the key initiatives and processes currently in place to tackle the proliferation and misuse of SALW. It looks first at relevant international agreements, then at regional initiatives, and finally at examples of inter-regional action.

The complex nature of the small-arms problem has been recognised as requiring action at the international as well as regional and national levels. Regional agreements and initiatives are important in the development of standards and practices that lay the foundations of international consensus. For example, current discussions at the international level about developing a common set of criteria to be taken into account when licensing aspects of SALW draw heavily on existing criteria identified in existing regional initiatives such as the EU Code of Conduct on Arms Sales and the Wassenaar Arrangement.

International initiatives

The United Nations Conference on the Illicit Trade in Small Arms in All its Aspects

The UN Conference was the first of its kind. The first time that all UN Member States had the opportunity to meet to discuss the illicit trade in SALW in all its aspects, it represented the first real attempt to agree a comprehensive set of measures to address the problem. There is no doubt that the conference has contributed to a better understanding of both the nature of the illicit trade in SALW and of the particular concerns and priorities of different countries and sub-regions.

The UN Conference was important for civil society in developing action to address SALW problems. The event put SALW firmly on the political agenda and provided a forum for civil society to demand change from governments. The Conference was also an important opportunity for government to hear the voices of those working to alleviate the suffering and pain caused by the illicit trade in SALW.

The conference was organised through the United Nations and took place at the UN headquarters in New York from 9 to 20 July 2001. It aimed to develop a framework for comprehensive action at the national, regional, and global levels to address the illicit trade in SALW in all its aspects: a framework commonly referred to as the UN Programme of Action (PoA).

Prior to the Conference, there were three Preparatory Committee meetings (Prep Coms), two of which considered drafts of the Programme of Action, which was eventually agreed at the end of the conference by consensus. Civil-society organisations from around the world were involved in all three preparatory meetings and during the conference itself. They undertook various roles, including advocacy, media work, and providing policy advice, and represented those working on a community level as well as those involved in policy development and research. The International Action Network on Small Arms (IANSA) performed a co-ordinating role for NGOs and civil-society groups and facilitated the participation of representatives from all regions of the world.

Many believed that the conference and the resulting Programme of Action were a missed opportunity for the international community to take lasting action to address the illicit trade in SALW in all its aspects. Certainly, although the Programme of Action that was agreed at the Conference provides an important set of standards and commitments, it does not tackle some of the key elements of the problem. There is no clear reference in the document to the issues of human rights, domestic gun control, and SALW transfers to non-State actors. There are also areas in which the PoA is very weak; they include criteria governing export controls, measures to ensure transparency, and international commitments on controlling the activities of arms brokers and on tracing lines of supply. However, following the conference there have been a range of positive initiatives undertaken by governments, particularly at the regional and sub-regional level, often involving civil-society organisations as key partners and drawing on the discussions at the conference and on the Programme of Action.

Box 14: Biting the bullet

Saferworld, International Alert, BASIC, and Bradford University developed the Biting the Bullet project in the period leading up to the UN Conference. The project worked with civil-society experts from around the world, producing 15 briefing papers on a range of issues relating to control of the illicit SALW trade.

Since the conference, Biting the Bullet has developed the project in three distinct areas. Firstly, in co-operation with IANSA, it aims to monitor implementation of the Programme of Action through the production of reports for the UN's Biennial Meetings and for a Review Conference in 2006. Secondly, it seeks to promote international understanding of issues that were not included in the Programme of Action, by hosting an Informal Consultative Group Process. Thirdly, it aims to contribute to the understanding of key policy subjects such as civilian possession and the implementation of embargoes.

The UN Programme of Action to Prevent, Combat and Eradicate the Illicit Trade in Small Arms and Light Weapons in All its Aspects

The Programme of Action is important because it provides a set of minimum standards and commitments which all States should adopt. It encourages further action from all States willing to develop more stringent commitments and comprehensive programmes. The Programme contains positive reference to the reduction of surplus stocks of small arms and the disposal of surplus weapons. It establishes clear international norms and encourages programmes to promote stockpile management. It contains provisions relating to the disarmament, demobilisation, and reintegration of ex-combatants. It explicitly calls on all States to co-operate with the enforcement of UN Security Council embargoes. And finally, importantly, the Programme of Action contains a commitment requiring States to authorise exports of SALW on the basis of strict national export criteria that are 'consistent with States' existing obligations under international law'.

Many of the commitments in the Programme of Action are much less comprehensive, however, and some issues were not addressed adequately at all in the final version. In addition to those mentioned above, the failure to address the proliferation of SALW associated with Licensed Production Overseas was disappointing, as was the omission of specific commitments on measures to enhance transparency. While the Programme of Action does make explicit reference in several places to the role of civil society in the process of implementation, it is still very much a State-oriented document.

The final UN Programme of Action was divided into four parts:

- Part I: *Preamble*. This outlined the context in which the document was agreed and included reference to the 'devastating consequences of SALW proliferation on women, children and the elderly'. It also made explicit reference to the importance of the role of civil society in '... assisting Governments to prevent, combat and eradicate the illicit trade in SALW'.
- Part II – *Preventing, combating, and eradicating the illicit trade in small arms and light weapons in all its aspects* – contained commitments to act at the national, regional, and global levels. This structure was to some degree based on that of previous initiatives, including the Bamako Declaration (see below).
- Part III contained commitments relating to *implementation, international co-operation, and assistance*, including specific commitments by States to 'ensure coordination, complementarity and synergy in efforts to deal with the illicit trade in SALW', and to provide technical and financial support to enable implementation.

- Part IV: *Follow-up to the UN Conference on the illicit trade in SALW in all its aspects.* This part contained the important commitment to convene a review conference not later than 2006 to review progress on implementation and to convene meetings on a biennial basis, 'to consider the national, regional and global implementation of the Programme of Action'. It also made commitments to consider developing an international instrument to trace SALW and to enhance co-operation in preventing, combating, and eradicating illicit brokering.

Box 15: Understanding the Programme of Action

To access the UN Programme of Action online in Arabic, Chinese, English, French, Russian, or Spanish, go to
http://disarmament.un.org/cab/Programme of Action.html

For a detailed critical analysis of the Programme of Action, see Biting the Bullet Briefing 15 – *Implementing the UN action programme for combating the illicit trafficking in small arms and light weapons in all its aspects* (available online at www.international-alert.org/publications.htm#security or by telephone or post from Saferworld – see contact details in Part 4 of this Handbook).

Follow-up to the UN Small Arms Conference and Implementation of the Programme of Action – The 2003 Biennial Meeting of States

Proposals to establish a mechanism for implementing the Programme were rejected at the Conference. As a result, in the final Programme of Action, most of the responsibility for implementation is left to States, which may voluntarily report to the UN Department for Disarmament Affairs on progress.

Agreement on organising biennial meetings and a review conference is therefore extremely important, because they provide opportunities for civil society to monitor implementation and argue for more sustainable and more effective action. To find out more about international civil-society action on implementation of the Programme of Action, contact the International Action Network on Small Arms (see contact details in Part 4 of this Handbook).

Box 16: Implementing the UN Programme of Action – civil society in action

The role of civil society in the implementation of the Programme of Action is explicit within its contents. Since July 2001, many civil-society organisations have been involved in various aspects of implementation, from involvement in the drafting of new legislation to performing vital roles in practical projects such as weapons collection and public-awareness programmes.

Civil-society organisations from all regions of the world have come together to work on a major project to monitor the implementation of the Programme of Action by all States. The International Action Network on Small Arms (IANSA) plans to publish an implementation report in advance of each Biennial Meeting of States (in 2003 and 2005) and in advance of the 2006 Review Conference. The first of these reports, produced by the Biting the Bullet project (Saferworld, Bradford University, and International Alert) and featuring contributions from more than 100 NGOs, academics, and others worldwide, has been produced to put pressure on governments to ensure that the Programme of Action is implemented fully and effectively.

This report, launched in June 2003, carries a strong message to governments that civil society is united in its desire to see lasting change to reduce the human cost of small-arms proliferation and misuse.

Protocol against the Illicit Manufacturing of and Trafficking in Firearms, Their Parts and Components and Ammunition, supplementing the Convention against Trans-national Organized Crime

The Protocol against the Illicit Manufacturing of and Trafficking in Firearms, Their Parts and Components and Ammunition, supplementing the Convention against Trans-national Organized Crime, was passed by the UN General Assembly on 31 May 2001. More commonly known as the UN Firearms Protocol or Vienna Protocol, the document was developed over a three-year period under the auspices of the Vienna-based UN Economic and Social Council (ECOSOC) Commission on Crime Prevention and Criminal Justice.

The prime focus of the Protocol is crime prevention and law enforcement. As such, its scope is narrower than that of (for instance) the UN Programme of Action. In addition, the Protocol exempts State-to-State transactions and State transfers made in the interest of national security; it focuses on crimes that are transnational in nature and involve organised criminal groups. Its provisions, if fully implemented, would put in place a number of very important measures to regulate the illicit manufacturing and trafficking of firearms. In so doing, it would also enhance co-operation, information exchange, and transparency.

The Protocol has yet to enter into force, because the requisite forty States have not ratified the document. Consequently, the key priority is to ensure that the State-signatories to the Protocol ratify the agreement as soon as possible. As a Treaty, the UN Firearms Protocol will legally bind its parties to implement all of its provisions. This is in contrast to the UN Small Arms Programme of Action, which is only politically binding. The entry into force of the Firearms Protocol will thus carry considerable weight and, if fully implemented, it should play a significant part in establishing an effective international system for the control of the illicit manufacturing and trafficking of firearms, their parts, components, and ammunition.

Some of the key elements of the UN Firearms Protocol include the following commitments:

- To adopt legislation to criminalise the illicit manufacturing and trafficking of firearms and the alteration or removal of markings from firearms.
- To introduce measures to confiscate, seize, and destroy or dispose of illicitly manufactured or trafficked firearms.
- To maintain records for 10 years of firearms markings and details of international firearms transactions.
- To ensure the detailed marking of firearms at the time of manufacture, on import, and when government firearms pass into civilian hands, so as to permit the identification by all States of the country of manufacture.
- To introduce a detailed system of export and import licensing and authorisation, and provisions relating to the international transit of firearms.
- To introduce provisions controlling the illicit reactivation of deactivated firearms.
- To introduce measures to detect, prevent, and eliminate the theft, loss, diversion, and illicit manufacture and trafficking of firearms.
- To consider establishing controls regulating brokering and brokers, including the registration of brokers and licensing of brokering transactions.
- To actively co-operate and exchange information.

The Wassenaar Arrangement

The Wassenaar Arrangement on Export Controls for Conventional Arms and Dual-Use Goods and Technologies was established in July 1996 to 'promote transparency and greater responsibility in transfers of conventional arms and dual-use technologies'.

The 33 current signatories to the Wassenaar Arrangement make up the majority of global arms manufacturers and exporters, including the USA, EU Member States, and a number of former Soviet Bloc Eastern European States, along with Argentina, Japan, New Zealand, South Korea, and Turkey. A key component of the Arrangement is the agreement by States to exchange information, on a voluntary basis, regarding the authorisation or refusal of transfers of certain types of controlled goods.

Although Wassenaar was originally concerned only with major conventional weapons and dual-use technologies, in December 2000 a meeting of Participating States in the Wassenaar Arrangement noted that States 'reaffirmed the importance of responsible export policies towards, and effective export controls over, small arms and light weapons to prevent destabilising accumulations'. In 2002, Wassenaar States agreed a set of best-practice guidelines and criteria for exports of SALW, under which, when considering proposed exports of SALW, participating States will take into account the following considerations, among others:

- the need to avoid destabilising accumulations of arms;
- the record of compliance of the recipient country with regard to international obligations and commitments;
- the goal of least diversion of human and economic resources to armaments;
- the right of nation States to exercise individual or collective self-defence;
- the respect for human rights and fundamental freedoms in the recipient country;
- the risk that the weapons might be used to support or encourage terrorism;
- the risk that the weapons might be used to prolong or aggravate an existing armed conflict; and
- the risk of diversion or inappropriate re-export.

Despite the efforts of some participants, there has as yet been no agreement on establishing a system of information exchange on SALW such as exists for major conventional weapons. It is to be hoped that SALW will be brought within the information-sharing mechanisms of the Arrangement.

Wassenaar States have, however, adopted a non-binding 'indicative list' of information to be incorporated in end-use assurances, which participating States may use at their discretion, including, among other matters:

- the identity of all parties involved in the transaction;
- a detailed description of the goods and their end-use; and
- an undertaking not to re-export or trans-ship the goods covered without approval from the originating government.

Wassenaar States have also identified 'best practice' on effective enforcement, including the examination of goods and documentation at point of export; the detention of suspect shipments and the seizure of unauthorised or illegal exports; and the monitoring of arrival at destination.

In 2002, a statement was agreed on an 'understanding of arms brokers', in which it was acknowledged that it was important for States to regulate arms-brokering activities, and that participating States should consider adopting measures such as requiring registration of arms brokers, or requiring licensing or authorisation of brokering.

For the full text of the Wassenaar Arrangement, visit www.wassenaar.org/ or http://projects.sipri.se/expcon/Wassenaar_documents.html

Regional initiatives

The Bamako Declaration on the African Common Position on the Illicit Proliferation, Circulation and Trafficking of Small Arms and Light Weapons

In July 1999 the 35th summit of the Organisation of African Unity (OAU), held in Algiers, called for an 'African common approach' to address problems related to the use, transfer, and illegal manufacturing of small arms and to develop a common African approach for the UN Conference on Small Arms in 2001.

In May 2000, the OAU convened the *First Continental Meeting of African Experts on Small Arms and Light Weapons* in Addis Ababa, Ethiopia. The meeting decided on the adoption of an African common position and agreed a set of recommendations (see below) for the adoption of policies, institutional arrangements, and operational measures for addressing the proliferation, circulation, and trafficking of small arms.

The ensuing Bamako Declaration, issued in Mali during the OAU ministerial meeting held in December 2000, called for co-ordinated action to control small-arms proliferation in Africa at the national, regional, and international levels. The Declaration – to which all members of the OAU (now African Union) are party – explicitly stated the wide-ranging and devastating impact that the uncontrolled proliferation of small arms and light weapons is having on the African continent.

In setting out commitments at the international, regional, and national levels, the Bamako Declaration established a blueprint which proved to be very influential in guiding discussions at the United Nations 2001 Small Arms Conference.

Civil-society actors contributed to the development of the Declaration, which makes reference to the involvement of civil-society organisations in the fight against small arms. Key elements of the declaration are as follows:

At the national level, States are committed to:

- strengthen or introduce legislation or regulations to curb the illicit manufacturing, trafficking, and illegal possession and use of small arms, light weapons, and ammunition and to prevent the breaching of international arms embargoes;
- introduce appropriate measures to control arms transfers by manufacturers, suppliers, traders, and brokers, as well as shipping and transit agents;
- work closely with civil society to help to develop national action plans to tackle the problem and to promote public awareness programmes on the problem of the proliferation and illicit trafficking of small arms and light weapons;
- encourage the voluntary surrender of illicit small arms and light weapons and the destruction of surplus, obsolete or confiscated weapons.

At the regional level, States are committed to:

- co-ordinate and harmonise legislation and controls over marking and record-keeping and controls governing imports, exports, and the licit trade;
- strengthen regional and continental co-operation and information exchange among police, customs, and border-control officials.

At the international level, States are committed to:

- encourage arms-supplying countries to recognise that trade in small arms should be limited to governments and duly authorised traders;
- introduce all necessary measures to regulate and control arms transfers by manufacturers, suppliers, traders, brokers, and shipping and transit agents, including exports of surplus weapons stocks to African countries.

The Bamako Declaration aims to ensure that action on small arms is co-ordinated across Africa. It is also an important guide and reference point for African States as they proceed with the complementary process of implementing the other key African agreements that have been concluded at the sub-regional level, including the ECOWAS Moratorium on the Importation, Exportation and Manufacture of Light Weapons; the Nairobi Declaration on the Problem of the Proliferation of

Illicit Small Arms and Light Weapons in the Great Lakes Region and the Horn of Africa; and the SADC Protocol on the Control of Firearms, Ammunition and Other Related Materials. Many of the commitments of the Bamako Declaration are similar to those contained in these sub-regional agreements. Indeed, in some cases these sub-regional agreements have built upon and go beyond the commitments of the Bamako Declaration.

Implementation of aspects of these sub-regional agreements (and consequently, therefore, of the Bamako Declaration's provisions) has begun, but the process has in many cases been slow. Addressing the small-arms problem is, however, a complex and long-term endeavour, and it will take time to reap the rewards of greater peace and stability that effective reduction of small-arms proliferation will bring. Concerted efforts are needed to ensure that the Bamako Declaration and these other sub-regional agreements are implemented quickly and effectively; there is a clear and important role for civil society in this process.

For the full text of the Bamako Declaration, visit
www.small-arms.co.za/Bamakodec01.html

SADC Protocol on the Control of Firearms, Ammunition and Other Related Materials

During the 1990s, the true impact of the uncontrolled proliferation of small arms and light weapons became increasingly apparent. International attention began to focus on its effect on security, stability, and sustainable development. The States of Southern Africa, which were and continue to be chronically affected by the scourge of small arms, decided that a concerted effort was needed to address its effects.

A Southern African Regional Action Programme on Light Arms and Illicit Trafficking was agreed in May 1998 and officially endorsed by Southern African Development Community (SADC) and European Union (EU) foreign ministers in November the same year. The Regional Action Programme takes a broad and integrated approach to the problem; it covers four key areas:

- combating illicit trafficking;
- strengthening regulation and controls on accumulation and transfers;
- promoting the removal of arms from society and the destruction of surplus arms; and
- enhancing transparency, information exchange, and consultation.

The Regional Action Programme laid the foundations for the agreement of the *Declaration concerning Firearms, Ammunition and other Related Materials in the SADC* (March 2001) and the *SADC Protocol on the Control of Firearms, Ammunition and Other Related Materials* (agreed in August 2001 and also known as the SADC Firearms Protocol). The SADC Firearms Protocol outlines key measures that the 14 States signatories are legally bound to fulfil. Key elements of the Protocol include the following:

- review and harmonisation of legislation governing the control of firearms;
- improvement of the operational capacity of law-enforcement agencies;
- collection, destruction, and disposal of firearms;
- awareness raising and public education on the impact of firearms on society;
- review of controls over State-owned firearms;
- review and improvement of firearms marking and tracing mechanisms; and
- provision of mutual legal assistance.

Within the SADC region, a co-ordinating body, the SADC Committee on Small Arms, has been established, and the Southern African Regional Police Chiefs Co-operation Organisation (SARPCCO) has been delegated as the implementing agency for work on the problems of small arms in the region. In addition, a SADC–EU Working Group on Small Arms meets regularly to work on co-operation between the two regions on small-arms issues.

Significant progress has been made by some of the countries of Southern Africa in implementing the SADC Protocol. Some of the priorities for implementation of the SADC Firearms Protocol include the following:

- establishment of National Focal Points – NFPs have been established in South Africa, Mozambique, Botswana and Tanzania;
- establishment of national electronic databases – Mauritius and South Africa are the only SADC States to have these at present;
- review and harmonisation of national firearms legislation – South Africa has agreed a new Firearms Act, and Tanzania and Botswana are currently reviewing their legislation;
- public awareness raising – the NGO 'Gun Free South Africa' has undertaken a lot of work in this area in South Africa, and the Christian Council of Mozambique has conducted education work through its weapons-collection project; and
- conduct of joint operations – the Operations Rachel conducted by South Africa and Mozambique to collect and destroy arms provide a good example for future joint operations.

For the text of the SADC Firearms Protocol, visit
www.sadc.int/ or
www.smallarmssurvey.org/RegionalDocs.html

The Nairobi Declaration on the Problem of the Proliferation of Illicit Small Arms and Light Weapons in the Great Lakes Region and the Horn of Africa

On 15 March 2000, government delegates from Burundi, the Democratic Republic of Congo (DRC), Djibouti, Ethiopia, Eritrea, Kenya, Rwanda, Sudan, Tanzania, and Uganda signed the Nairobi Declaration.

As in Southern Africa, the Declaration seeks to provide a broad approach to the challenges of small-arms proliferation in the region, focusing on measures to

- strengthen and harmonise legislation governing the control of firearms;
- strengthen the operational capacity of law-enforcement agencies;
- increase cross-border co-operation between law-enforcement agencies;
- collect and destroy weapons;
- enhance the demobilisation and re-integration of ex-combatants;
- improve police–community relations; and
- enhance public education and awareness raising.

A sub-regional body to co-ordinate and share information on the implementation of the Nairobi Declaration has been established. This body, the Nairobi Secretariat, based in the Kenyan capital, has a small staff responsible for ensuring the dissemination of information, co-ordination of activities, and enhanced co-operation between States in the sub-region.

A Co-ordinated Agenda for Action and accompanying Implementation Plan were concluded in November 2000, detailing the specific requirements for the Declaration's implementation. In August 2002 the First Ministerial Review Conference of the Nairobi Declaration took place, and an updated implementation plan was elaborated, creating a timetable for action. In addition, a number of donor agencies have formed a group known as the Friends of Nairobi to support the Declaration's implementation.

The Ministerial Review Conference sought to re-invigorate the implementation of the Nairobi Declaration, a process which until then had been moving slowly. Some of the key priorities for implementation reflect those areas where progress still needs to made. They include:

- establishment of National Focal Points (NFPs);
- operationalisation of the Nairobi Secretariat and ensuring that it will play the active role envisaged in the Nairobi Declaration;
- conduct of research on the small-arms problem in the region;
- exchange of information between NFPs and other actors;
- establishment of national firearms databases;
  and

- creation of national action plans. To date, national action plans have been developed by Tanzania and are under development in Uganda and Kenya.

Civil society has been engaged throughout the development of the Nairobi Declaration and is now supporting the implementation of the Declaration's provisions. For example, a large number of local civil-society organisations are members of their respective National Focal Points. For instance, People With Disabilities, Centre for Conflict Resolution, Oxfam GB, and Uganda Joint Christian Council are members of Uganda's NFP.

For the text of the Nairobi Declaration, visit
www.globalpolicy.org/security/smallarms/regional/nairobi.htm
or www.smallarmssurvey.org/RegionalDocs.html

The ECOWAS Moratorium on the Import, Export and Manufacture of Small Arms and Light Weapons in West Africa

In October 1998, the heads of the 16 Member States of the Economic Community of West African States signed the *ECOWAS Moratorium on Import, Export and Manufacture of Small Arms and Light Weapons in West Africa*. The three-year renewable moratorium, which was extended in 2001 for a further three years, was the first of its kind. West Africa was consequently the first region in the world to declare a moratorium on small arms and light weapons. The ECOWAS moratorium is seen by many to be one of the first agreements to define small-arms proliferation in terms of a 'security first' approach, in which integrated measures to control small arms were seen as a vital pre-requisite for long-term, peaceful, sustainable development.

This political declaration was an important first step for regional action to combat the proliferation of small arms. It has received international approval from (for example) the members of the Wassenaar Arrangement, who offered unqualified support for the agreement and stated that they would respect the provisions of the Moratorium within national export controls and would provide advisory and/or technical assistance to help its implementation.

In 1998, a Plan of Action was developed by ECOWAS members to implement the Moratorium. Following this, the UNDP Programme for Coordination and Assistance for Security and Development (PCASED) was established to provide technical assistance for an initial period of five years. It identified the following key priorities requiring assistance:

- improved controls at harbours, airports, and border crossings;
- reforming military, security, and police forces through regional training programmes;
- collection and destruction of weapons;

- co-operation with civil-society organisations;
- establishing dialogue with arms manufacturers;
- establishing a data-bank and a small-arms register in West Africa.

At the 1999 ECOWAS Summit, the heads of government endorsed the principle of a regional arms register, thus preparing the way for implementation, and also adopted a Code of Conduct which sets out steps that governments and the ECOWAS Secretariat should take in order to make the Moratorium more effective. These include establishing national commissions and regional focal points, and offering more support within ECOWAS to manage implementation of the moratorium. The Code of Conduct sets out a plan to support governments in implementing the national requirements of the Moratorium and building the capacity of ECOWAS to manage and extend the agreement. As a binding agreement, the Code of Conduct sets out concrete actions to be taken by the Member States to implement the moratorium and provides a framework for the ECOWAS States to adhere to their commitments to the goal of the Moratorium.

For the text of the ECOWAS Moratorium, visit www.nisat.org/ or www.smallarmssurvey.org/RegionalDocs.html

Inter-American Convention Against the Illicit Manufacturing of and Trafficking in Firearms, Ammunition, Explosives and Other Related Materials and the Model Regulations for the Control of the International Movement of Firearms, Their Parts and Components, and Ammunition

The Inter-American Convention is the only legally binding regional agreement that deals with firearms proliferation in the context of law enforcement and crime control. All Member States of the Organisation of American States (OAS), with the exception of Dominica, have signed the agreement; at the time of writing, 19 had reached the point of ratification.[70]

The Convention broadly defines firearms as *'any barrelled weapon which will or is designed to or may be readily converted to expel a bullet or projectile by the action of an explosive – any other weapons or destructive device such as an explosive, incendiary or gas bomb, grenade, rocket launcher, missile, missile system or mine'*. The breadth of this definition is a principal strength of the Inter-American Convention. While in some other forums the range of weapons covered under such definitions is much more limited, the Inter-American Convention can be applied to the range of small arms and light weapons responsible for death, injury, and trauma in the western hemisphere. The aims of the Convention are to

- criminalise illicit manufacturing and trafficking;
- mark weapons at manufacture and import;
- establish an effective licensing system to govern exports, imports, and transits;

- strengthen controls at export points;
- exchange information on producers, dealers, importers and exporters, routes and techniques used in illicit trafficking; and
- exchange experience and training in areas such as identification, detection, tracing, and intelligence gathering.

Prior to the UN Conference, in May 2001, the Consultative Committee of the Inter-American Convention met in Washington DC to approve the work programme for 2001–2002, and to review the ratifications of the Convention, discuss the case study presented by the government of Mexico, and identify points of contact within each national government, as well as central authorities responsible for the legal and legislative aspects of ratification, adoption, and implementation. The 2001–2002 work programme includes the following key activities, among others:

- Encourage participation, by all convention signatories, in the questionnaire approved at the First Meeting of Parties to the Convention. As of 15 June 2001, only 16 of the 33 signatories to the Convention had responded to the questionnaire, which allows for bureaucratic, technical, and political monitoring and follow up.
- Update the inventory of measures adopted by States, as indicated in the above-mentioned questionnaire.
- Create private e-mail lists for sharing information among national entities and central authorities.
- Develop a register of arms suppliers within the OAS region.
- Formalise contacts and relationships with the UN, European Union (EU), and other international organisations interested in multilateral co-operation.
- Publish a Convention website with various levels of private and public access.
- Invite States to develop and present case studies, such as the one presented by Mexico in May 2001, regarding the illegal arms trafficking environment and the status of Convention ratification and implementation.
- Advance the development of model legislation needed to implement the Convention, but not contemplated in CICAD Model Regulations (see discussion below).

CICAD Model Regulations

Concurrent with the Inter-American Convention negotiations, the OAS Member States also formulated a set of practical guidelines to complement the effective implementation of the Convention. Developed under the auspices of CICAD, the

Inter-American Drug Abuse Control Commission, the Model Regulations were also adopted in November 1997. These Model Regulations consist of a series of harmonised measures and procedures for monitoring and controlling the international movement of commercially traded firearms, their parts and components among OAS States that have adopted the regulations, together with guidelines for minimum standards required for harmonised licensing. They also outline proposals for record keeping and information sharing on imports and exports, including the quantity, type, and serial numbers of firearms.

These regulations contain three key weaknesses which make it difficult to fully prevent small arms from entering the illicit market. First, the Model Regulations are not directly connected to the Inter-American Convention and apply only to OAS Member States who adopt them. When a manufacturer or broker from an OAS Member State sells firearms to brokers and buyers from non-compliant OAS States, or non-members with lax controls and regulations, there is a danger that these arms will enter the illicit market.

Second, the Convention and Model Regulations are limited to commercially traded firearms, leaving State-to-State transfers of small arms to a variety of military, security, and police end-users inadequately regulated. A further gap in controls exists with regard to State transfers of arms to non-State actors. The end-product of the UN Conference indicates that there is still a lack of political will, both inside and outside the OAS, to take aggressive action on these two aspects of government-sanctioned transfers.

Third, the adoption and the implementation of the Model Regulations are not well co-ordinated with other inter-American agreements and implementing organs, such as those aimed at fighting corruption. For this reason the Model Regulations do not take advantage of potential synergies with other relevant regional initiatives.

For the full text of the OAS Convention, visit
www.oas.org/juridico/english/treaties/a-63.html

OSCE Document on Small Arms and Light Weapons

On 24 November 2000, the Organisation for Security and Co-operation in Europe (OSCE) adopted a Document on Small Arms and Light Weapons which sets out norms, principles, and measures to address the proliferation of SALWs. It recognises the 'excessive and destabilising accumulation of the uncontrolled spread of small arms' and aims to improve regional security across the 55 participating States from Europe, Central Asia, and North America (see endnote for full list of OSCE Member States).[71] The document includes statements relating to national controls on the manufacture of small arms; marking, tracing, and accurate record-keeping of small arms; increased transparency measures relating to national marking systems; and controls on the export and import of SALWs. It also reflects a recognition of the impact of small arms on the OSCE's role in conflict prevention and democracy building.[72]

The scope of the measures contained in the document is variable, revealing both its strengths and weaknesses. For example, throughout the document there is a clear acknowledgement that export controls on legal transfers are crucial in combating the illicit SALW trade. The adoption of commonly agreed standards (based on the *Principles Governing Conventional Arms Transfers* adopted by the Forum for Security Co-operation on 25 November 1993)[73] for licensing transfers of SALW requires States Parties to consider several criteria prior to deciding whether to grant or revoke an export-licence application. These include respect for human rights, the internal and regional situation of the country, and compliance with international obligations. Accordingly, States Parties 'will avoid' licensing exports where, for instance, SALW might be used for 'the violation or suppression of human rights and fundamental freedoms' or 'threaten the national security of other states'.[74] However, although the criteria represent a comprehensive set of principles (drawing on the criteria of the EU Code of Conduct on Arms Exports), the wording is ambiguous and open to interpretation, which contributes to considerable variance in implementation.

In February 2003, an international seminar was held in Bucharest, Romania, to examine implementation of the OSCE Document and the UN Programme of Action on SALW. States agreed to identify and develop guides to best practice on various aspects of small-arms policy and practice at the national level, to advance common standards among all States. These aspects include controls on arms-brokering activities, procedures for stockpile management and security, and export and import policy. While establishing best practices and standards common to all States is an important norm-building activity, implementation and enforcement are undertaken at the national level, where they are subject to the political will, commitment, and capacity of individual States.

The OSCE Document is limited in several respects:

- Adoption and application is voluntary, so commitments are politically binding rather than legally binding.
- Commitments are confined to participating States and are thus not applicable to transfers between OSCE States and non-OSCE States.
- With the risk of diversion of SALW to unauthorised end-users, 'the development of common measures on import, export and transit procedures should be seen as an area for urgent government action'.[75]
- Standards are open to interpretation, and consequently implementation may vary considerably.

- There are no provisions relating to regulating domestic/civilian possession of SALW.

Despite its limitations, and problems associated with implementation, the Document is a useful contribution to regional and international efforts to combat the proliferation of small arms. It was also a particularly important contribution to the development of the UN Programme of Action.

For the full text of the OSCE Document, visit www.osce.org/docs/english/fsc/2000/decisions/fscew231.htm

European Union Code of Conduct on Arms Exports

The EU Code of Conduct, agreed in June 1998, stemmed from an initiative proposed by France and the United Kingdom. It was developed in part as a response to calls for a more responsible approach to exports of arms, including SALW, and, in part, as an effort to adopt a harmonised approach to weapons transfers within the 15-nation European Union.

The Code aims to set 'high common standards which should be regarded as the minimum for the management of, and restraint in conventional arms transfers by all EU Member States'. It outlines the common principles, such as transparency and accountability, which underpin future EU arms transfers. Civil-society organisations from across the EU were instrumental in the development of the concept of the Code of Conduct and in creating the favourable political environment in which it was agreed.

Criteria and operative provisions

The Code includes guidelines previously detailed under the eight criteria on conventional arms transfers agreed in Lisbon and Luxembourg in 1991 and 1992, which address the following considerations:

- respect for international commitments of EU Member States in areas such as embargoes, treaties, and control regimes;
- respect for human rights in the country of final destination;
- the internal situation in the country of final destination;
- preservation of regional peace, security, and stability;
- the national security interests of the Member States and of allied countries;
- the behaviour and attitudes of the buyer country with regard to terrorism and respect for international law;
- the risk of diversion or re-export of equipment within the buyer country; and

- the compatibility of arms exports with the technical and economic capacity of the recipient country.

The EU Code also includes 'operative provisions', a basic system for all Member States to exchange information on those applications for arms-export licences which are denied, and limited consultations to discourage undercutting (i.e. where one Member State approves an application which has already been refused by another). It also provides for an Annual Review of the implementation of the Code.

The EU Code was important for many reasons, not least that it created the opportunity to develop lines of communication between EU governments. Now, five years after the Code was agreed, the information provided through denial notifications is apparently proving a revelation to many EU Member States, fostering reciprocal understanding of the implementation of the Code criteria. The regime has also been successful in attracting the support of a number of countries outside the EU, and has been endorsed by a number of other States, including Canada and the EU associate nations. The Code will assume even greater significance in 2004, when 10 new States will join the EU, raising membership to 25 (see endnote for a full list of current members and the 10 States due to join in 2004).[76] The USA has endorsed the Code with specific regard to transfers of SALW.

The experience of negotiating the Code has also prompted review, by EU governments, of some other aspects of their arms-control regimes, and the EU Code Annual Review process has led to Member States addressing within the context of the Code a number of issues untouched by the Code itself. It is expected that this process will continue to provide for the evolution of the role and implementation of the EU Code. For example, EU Member States have:

- proposed a mechanism for controlling exports of non-military equipment that may be used for internal repression (2001);
- agreed a set of guidelines for controlling arms brokers, and commenced negotiations on a Common Position on arms brokering (2002);
- begun to address the issue of the overseas production of military goods under licence (2002);
- agreed a common core of elements that should be found in a certificate of final destination (2002);
  and
- decided to extend the denial notification mechanism to provide for some sharing of information with EU Associate Countries (2002).

Civil-society organisations have been central in monitoring implementation of the Code, and in putting pressure on governments to widen its scope. These activities have included the development of an EU Campaign in 2003, which calls for adoption of the Code's provisions into national law by Member States and for the development of effective controls on the activities of arms brokers.

For the full text text of the EU Code of Conduct, visit http://projects.sipri.se/expcon/eucode.htm

European Union Joint Action on Small Arms

In an effort to contribute to global efforts to tackle small-arms proliferation, the EU Council of Ministers adopted in December 1998 a Joint Action on the EU's contribution to combating the destabilising accumulation and spread of small arms and light weapons. This agreement, which builds on the EU Programme for Preventing and Combating Illicit Trafficking in Conventional Arms adopted by the Council in June 1997, and the EU Code of Conduct on Arms Exports adopted in June 1998, takes a regional and incremental approach to the problem. The Joint Action, which listed 10 categories of small arms and light weapons, was amended in 2002 to include SALW ammunition within its provisions.

The Joint Action aims to further the international effort to combat the excessive and uncontrolled spread of small arms through support for existing regional and international initiatives. EU Member States agreed to develop a co-operative policy, concentrating on the following measures:

- combating and contributing to measures aimed at ending the destabilising accumulation and spread of small arms;
- contributing to the reduction of existing accumulations to levels consistent with countries' legitimate security needs;
- helping to solve the problems associated with accumulations of weapons; and
- making a multifaceted contribution to a range of control and reduction measures.

The EU Council publishes an annual report on the implementation of the Joint Action, incorporating activities undertaken as part of the EU Programme on Combating Illicit Trafficking in Conventional Arms. The most recent report, published in December 2002, detailed a wide range of activities carried out by Member States with regard to SALW. These included the following:

- Support for arms collection and/or destruction programmes in Albania, Bosnia and Herzegovina, Cambodia, East Timor, Kosovo, Macedonia, Niger, and Sierra Leone.
- Projects to build law-enforcement capacity in Guatemala, Honduras, Kenya, Mozambique, Nicaragua, and Romania.
- Support for soldier demobilisation and reintegration projects in Angola, Democratic Republic of Congo, Guinea-Bissau, Liberia, Sierra Leone, and Uganda.

- Financial support for civil society and NGOs working to address the problems caused by destabilising accumulations and the proliferation of small arms and light weapons.

The website of the European Union Joint Action on Small Arms is at

http://projects.sipri.se/expcon/eu_documents.html

5 Summary

Part 1 of the handbook has introduced the major elements of the small-arms policy context. It aimed to provide the user with an introduction to tackling the following questions:

- What are SALW?
- What is a small-arms transfer?
- What are the effects of SALW proliferation and misuse?
- What are the measures required to address factors driving demand for SALW, and what is needed to control the supply?
- What initiatives are already in place at the international and national levels to address the problems of small-arms proliferation and misuse?

There are many opportunities for civil-society organisations and others to take real and lasting action to resolve SALW problems. Existing initiatives such as the UN Programme of Action provide a framework within which to work. But an important role of civil society is also to act outside the parameters set by governments and others, to challenge decision makers to do more – and do it more effectively. Parts 2 and 3 of this book aim to help users to identify the aspects of the SALW on which they could take action, and to organise their action to ensure that it is as effective as possible.

Part 2
Planning for action

Contents

Introduction

An overview of planning

Good planning is essential to successful and sustainable action. Good planning enables you to maximise your opportunities and reduce the risk of failure. It provides you with a framework for developing, implementing, and evaluating action; it helps you to make the best use of scarce time and resources; and above all it ensures that your action is defined and driven by a clear purpose.

However, planning can sometimes become complicated and difficult to manage. One way to keep it simple is to break it down into stages. This part of the handbook introduces an approach to help you to develop relevant and focused responses to the problems that you face. It can be adopted at various levels of detail, depending on the length and breadth of the action that you aim to undertake. The process can be divided into six phases, listed below. Each phase is reduced to steps which, used sequentially, will help you to develop your plans and strategies for action.

There are always many activities that you might undertake in response to a particular situation. Planning provides a rational basis for choosing those activities that are likely to be most effective. The phases described below are designed to build on one another. However, it is not necessary to follow the entire process without deviation. You should use only the elements that apply to your own context.

Phase 1: Assessing the situation

Phase 2: Establishing goals

Phase 3: Developing a strategy

Phase 4: Planning the activity

Phase 5: Implementation and monitoring

Phase 6: Evaluation

Each of the six phases of planning represents a distinct stage in an organisation's preparation for action. Figure 2.1 indicates in general terms the sequence in which the process is approached. However, at all stages, it is important to look back to ensure that you keep your work focused on achieving the changes that you want to achieve. All phases of the planning cycle are important. They will help to inform your choice of action, to ensure that you act in the most effective way at the right time.

Figure 2.1: The planning cycle

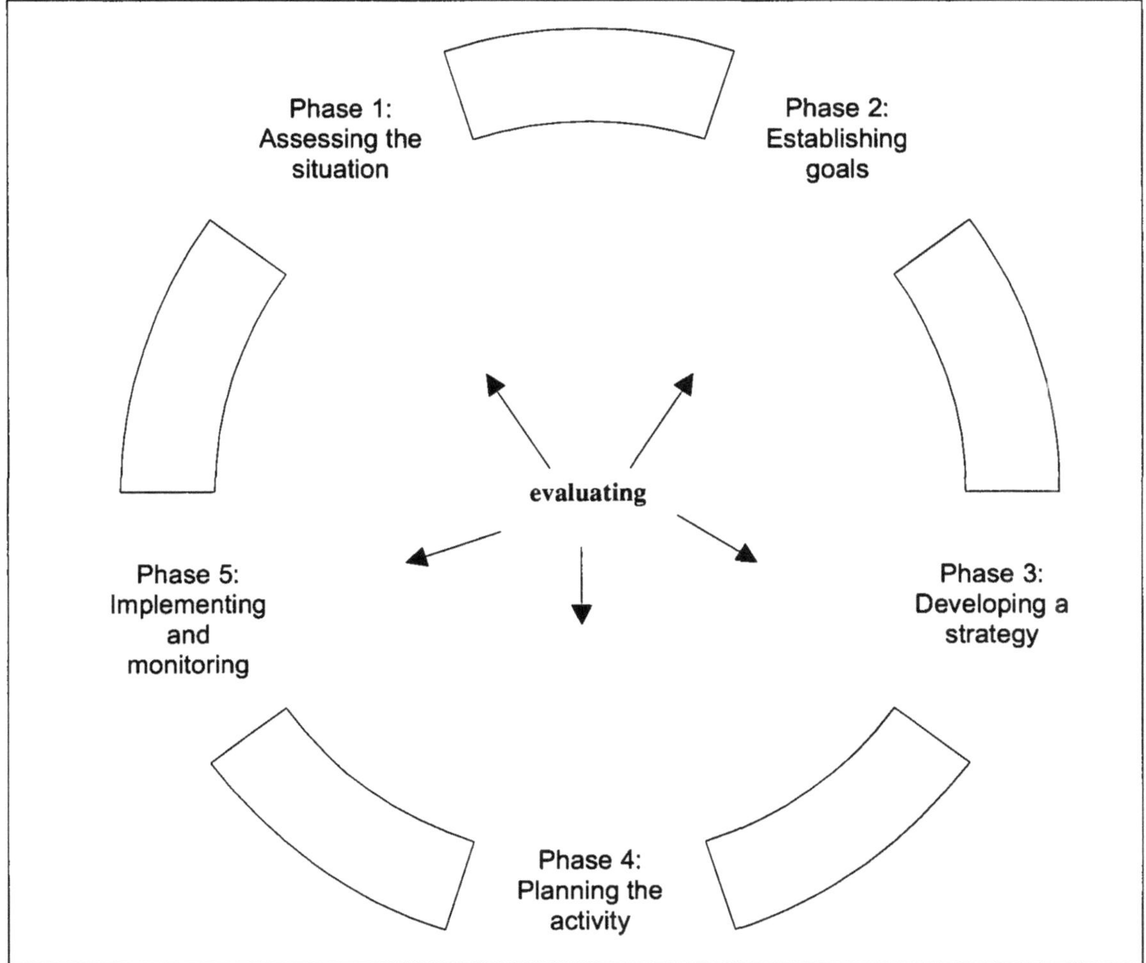

Participatory planning

Analysing your situation is the basis of good planning. It involves reflecting on the problems that you face, and identifying the best means to tackle them. Involving a wide range of people in the process should improve your planning, for the following reasons:

- The planning process should be a learning experience during which participants reach an improved common understanding of their problems and commit themselves to working towards a common goal.
- The more people you involve, and the more contributions that the process stimulates, the better the range of options and ideas that you are likely to identify.

- Involving those who will be responsible for implementing the plans helps to ensure that the plans are realistic, based on the full range of available strengths, and likely to help you to consider the role that each will play when taking action.

In each phase we introduce participatory planning tools that are designed to help you to develop your analysis. Each tool is briefly introduced and illustrated with an example.

Figure 2.2: How Part 2 fits with the rest of the handbook

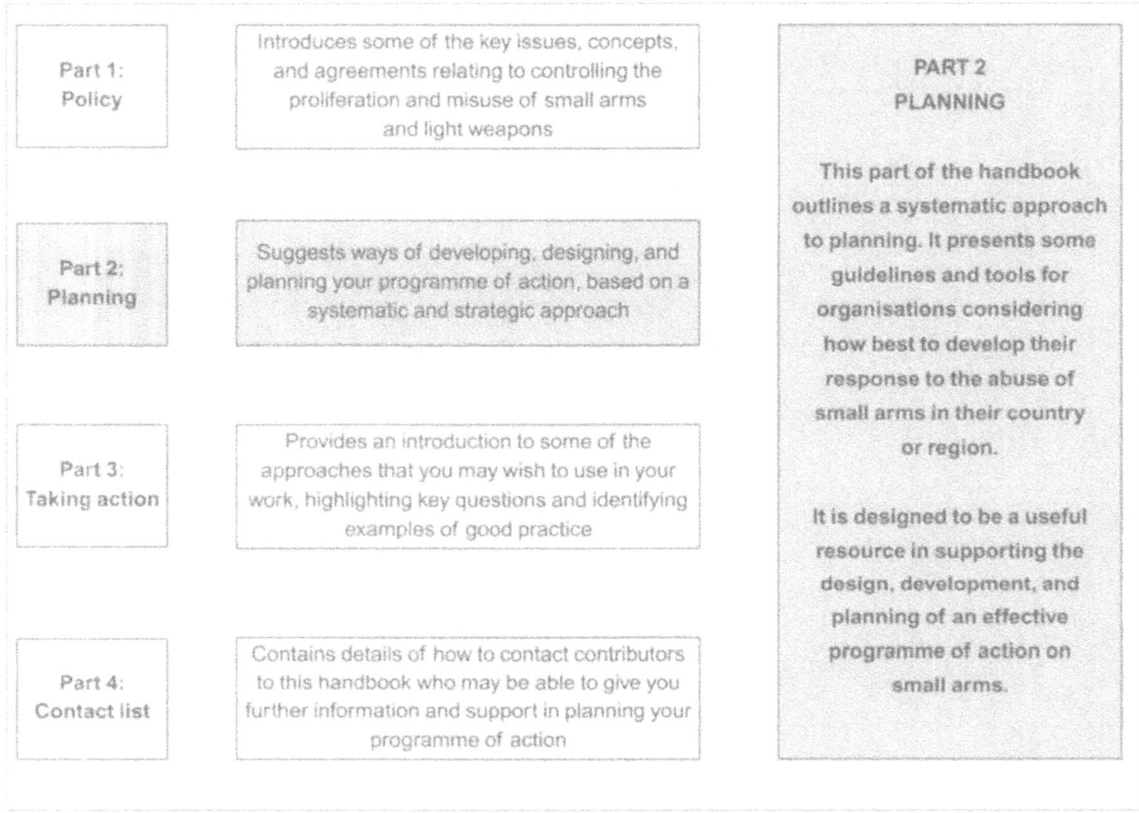

How to use the planning tools in a training or planning workshop

Each of the tools listed in Table 2.1 is featured in the planning process described in this part of the handbook. They are presented in the form of handouts which can be photocopied and used independently. The handouts are identified by the presence of a tinted line down the side of the page.

Table 2.1: Using the right tools and techniques at the right time

Tool or technique	Most useful for …	In which phase of the planning cycle is this included?
Problem and solution tree	Understanding problems and solutions as part of assessing the situation	Phase 1
Solutions table	Outlining the range of solutions available to you	Phase 1
SWOT analysis	Analysing the environment as part of assessing the situation	Phase 1
Ranking solutions	Prioritising solutions as part of establishing goals	Phase 2
Framing the issue	Building support for your work, both internally and externally	Phase 3
Forcefield analysis	Identifying stakeholders as part of developing strategy	Phase 3
Channels of influence: a matrix	Devising an influencing strategy	Phase 3
Influence map	Devising an influencing strategy	Phase 3
Timeline	Developing an action plan	Phase 4
Setting indicators	Implementing and monitoring your programme	Phase 5

The tools presented in this part of the handbook are designed to help you to understand the various elements involved in developing effective strategies and action plans. They are usually best used to facilitate group planning. Many of them contain an element of brainstorming, which is done best with others as a group exercise.

You can use the activity sheets associated with the tools either to facilitate discussion with an experienced planning group, or for training a group that is new to planning techniques.

> **The golden rules of brainstorming**
>
> **Nothing is wrong – question nothing – put everything down on paper.**
>
> When the exercise is complete, it is time to go back, test ideas more rigorously, and select the ones that are most relevant, workable, and likely to succeed.

Although every situation is different, the following guidelines should help you to use the worksheets most effectively:

- Participants should be divided into groups, consisting ideally of 4–7 people.
- Each activity is designed to be completed in about one hour.
- Hand out the activity sheets to each member of the group and ask one person to fill it in on behalf of the whole group.
- Another member of the group should be designated as time-keeper to ensure that people do not waste time on irrelevant details.

Notes on organising a training workshop[1]

Training should be well planned; preparation is vital. Box 16 lists questions to consider.

Box 17: Why, who, when, where, what for, what, and how?

Why?	• What are the aims and objectives of the training course or programme?
	• Are they realistic in terms of what the training can achieve?
Who?	• Who should attend?
	• Who will provide administrative and logistical support?
When?	• What time best suits the group and its members' needs?
	• How much time should be allowed for socialising, networking, and relaxing?
Where?	• Find a venue that is available, convenient, and within budget.
What for?	• What is the gap between what people know and what they need to know in order to be effective in their work?
What?	• Based on the course or programme objectives, what will the contents of the training be?
How?	• What training methods will you use?

Most of the exercises in this manual are based on a series of 'closed' questions, requiring specific, formal answers. These help the group to maintain its focus when dealing in a limited time with a complicated process. But as part of a training programme, these sessions would need to be interspersed with activities that stimulate creativity – such as brainstorming and role plays – with no pre-determined outcome. Different people have different learning styles, so it is important to introduce variety into any training course.

Role of the workshop facilitator

Facilitating is a skill which requires an ability to listen, an understanding of group dynamics, and the ability to encourage respect and understanding within the group. In most cases, ideally, there should be at least two facilitators working together, to share ideas and workload. They will have practical responsibilities, in addition to listening to and observing the group and dealing constructively with any problems that arise. Facilitators' responsibilities include the following:

- setting clear programme objectives
- providing clear instructions to participants
- providing materials
- keeping to time
- encouraging balanced participation
- asking provocative questions to encourage new lines of thinking
- providing real examples to illustrate successful uses of the tools
- offering additional personal experiences to less experienced group members

Figure 2.3: The six phases of planning

PHASE	KEY QUESTIONS TO ADDRESS	STEPS INVOLVED
Phase 1 – assessing the situation	What is the context that you are operating in, and what strengths do you bring to meet the challenge of that context?	Understanding problems & solutions Mapping solutions Analysing the environment Analysing your strengths & weaknesses
Phase 2 – establishing your goals	What kind of change are you seeking, and who needs to make the change?	Prioritising solutions Setting goals
Phase 3 – developing your strategy	How can you most effectively influence those who need to change?	Framing the issue Identifying stakeholders Devising an influencing strategy
Phase 4 – planning the activity	Who will do what and when?	Setting objectives Developing an action plan
Phase 5 - implementing and monitoring	Are you doing the right things at the right times, and are they working?	Implementing programmes and monitoring
Phase 6 – evaluating	What have you achieved and learned, and what should you do differently in future?	Evaluation

Phase 1: Assessing the situation

Introduction

This phase includes the following steps:

- Understanding problems and solutions
- Mapping solutions
- Analysing the environment

It is always tempting to start by taking action immediately. But if you want your action to be targeted and effective, it is worth taking time to identify what kind of action is likely to be most successful. The starting point for this is to understand the situation in which you are working.

This phase in the process is important in enabling you to use limited resources most effectively, for the following reasons.

- Unless you have a common and clear understanding of the problems that you face, as well as their causes, consequences, and possible solutions, you may soon find that you are unclear about what it is exactly that you are trying to change, how and why.
- Unless you take into account the factors – both internal and external – that may either help or hinder your work, you could find that your programme of action encounters difficulties that you had failed to predict.

Once you have considered the situation in which you plan to act, you are in a much better position to be clear about and consider further what you can achieve.

Understanding problems and their solutions

Before you take action, it is important to understand in some detail the problems that you face, and their causes. This will help you to decide where you should focus your efforts in addressing them. Ask yourself the following questions.

Key questions to address

What is the issue that we face?

What are the underlying causes?

- In other words, why does this problem exist? What are the roots of the problem?

What are the consequences?

For instance:

- What are the consequences of small-arms proliferation in terms of public health?
- What are the development and environmental consequences?
- What are the humanitarian consequences?

How could the causes of the problems be tackled, and what would the outcomes be if this were to happen?

- How has related change come about in the past?
- What can we learn from this?

One tool to help you to answer these questions is a Problem and Solution Tree (see Planning Tool 1).

Planning Tool 1: Problem and Solution Tree

Problem and Solution Trees can help you to assess a situation. See the example below, prepared by participants from FIQ, an NGO based in Kosovo, at a seminar on small arms organised by Saferworld in January 2003.

Context

Understanding problems and identifying their solutions is the starting point for action. It is vital to have a good understanding of the problems that you face, as well as their causes, consequences, and possible solutions. Without it, any organisation may soon become unclear about some of the fundamentals of its programme – what it is trying to change, how, and why.

Purpose

Analysis of situations affected by the proliferation and misuse of small arms invariably reveals a very complex set of inter-related causes and consequences. This realisation may be overwhelming and make it difficult to know where to start. Problem and Solution Trees are a tool to help you to outline the problems that your society faces, their causes and consequences, and then to use this analysis as a basis for developing a positive response to the situation. They provide a way of representing complex issues more simply and identifying ways of addressing seemingly intractable problems.

Method

Allow approximately 45 minutes for this exercise. It is ideally done by a mixed group of 5–10 people. If greater numbers are involved, consider dividing participants into small groups, which will each report back at the end. To construct the problem tree:

1. State the problem as an issue to be addressed.
2. Identify the main causes of the problem; name them in boxes below the problem statement.
3. Identify the main consequences of the problem; name them in boxes above the problem statement.

Then begin the solution tree:

4 For every cause of the problem already identified, suggest a solution; write this (maybe using a post-it note or a sticker) over the cause.

5 Consider what would be different if these solutions were achieved: how would the consequences be transformed? Identify the new outcomes. Write these (on post-it notes or stickers) over the consequences.

6 Finally, using the information from the previous step, construct a new tree. Above the line identify the new outcomes; below it, write the solutions; and through the middle, restate the same problem/issue in terms of your vision for the future.

Next step

The next step is to use the solutions that you have identified as a basis for setting your goals, as outlined in Phase 2: Establishing Goals.

Example of a Problem and Solution Tree: developing a small-arms campaign programme in Kosovo

The following example was produced by members of the Forum for Civic Initiative (FIQ-FCI) in Ferizaj, Kosovo during a planning workshop in January 2003 to identify opportunities for developing a programme of action against the abuse of small arms.

In the first tree, one major problem faced by FIQ is described in the middle box: the fact that in Kosovo the proliferation and abuse of small arms is not a matter of public concern. This was the problem that FIQ decided to analyse in greater depth. They did so by listing some of the main causes of the problem below the statement, and listing the consequences above it.

Then the group reviewed the initial problem statement ('Small arms is not a public issue') and in the second tree they restated this problem in positive terms, expressed in the form of what they wanted to achieve: their vision ('To make small arms a matter of public concern'). Then the group thought again about the causes of the problem already identified and considered how each in turn could be addressed and resolved. These solutions were added to the solutions tree below the vision statement. Finally, FIQ considered how, if these solutions were implemented, the outcomes would be different from those consequences identified in the problem analysis.

This process can be useful in developing a better understanding of a situation and beginning to think about possible solutions.

Figure 2.4: Problem and Solution Tree, produced by FIQ, Kosovo

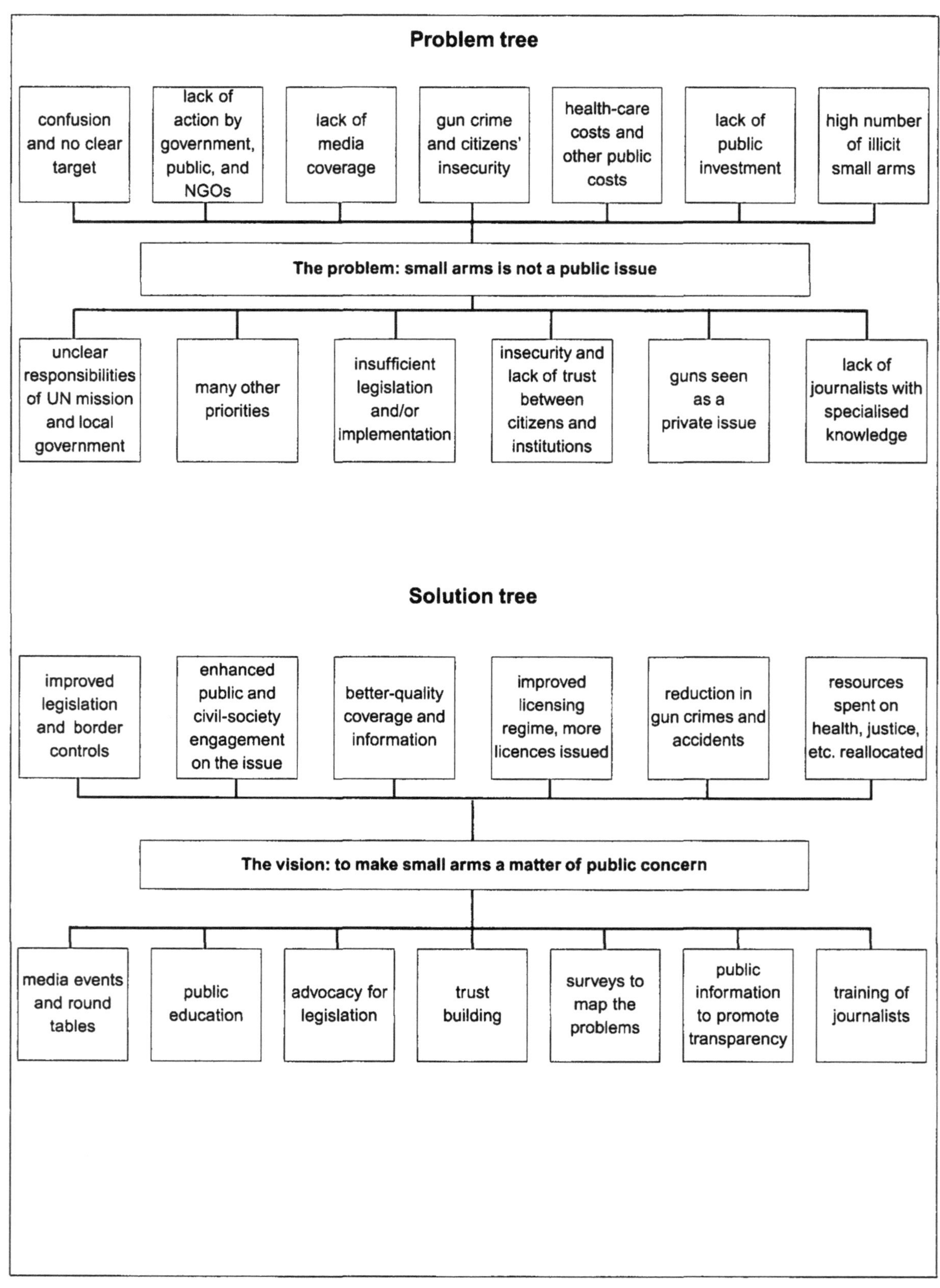

Figure 2.5: Template for a Problem and Solution Tree

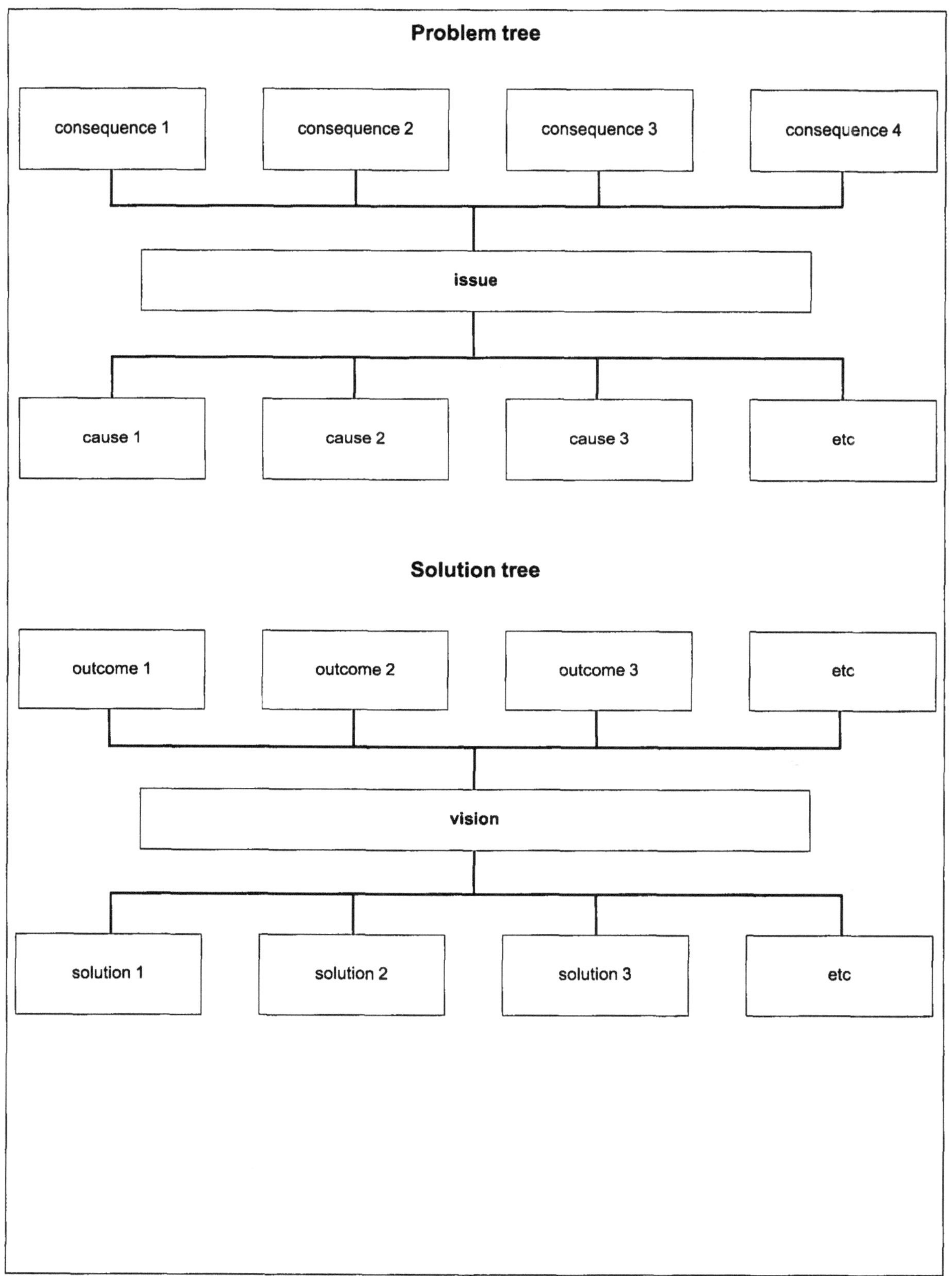

Mapping solutions

You should aim to be very clear about the range of possible solutions available to you before you start to develop your programme of action. This will put you in a position where you can make informed judgements about the best ways to proceed, and the various levels at which you will need to act.

Key questions to address

At what levels does change need to happen?

- at the local level?
- at the national level?
- at the regional level?
- at the international level?

What kind of change do we want to achieve at these different levels?

- A change in institutional policy, for example a government introducing new legislation on the possession of arms by civilians?
- A change in institutional practice, for example the establishment of a community-based gun-amnesty scheme?
- A change in the attitudes and opinions that members of the public, or a particular group, hold about an issue, for example changing public opinion to support a ban on handguns?
- A change in the way that members of the public, or a particular group (for instance men or women) act, for example voluntary demobilisation of rebel forces?

Who needs to change at each of these levels?

Is it for instance...

- an institution (the police, for example)?
- an individual or group within an institution (for instance, the Chief of Police or local police station chiefs)?
- key individuals in society (for instance, opinion formers such as editors of popular media)?
- a social group or members of a social group within the wider public (for instance, young men living in a particular geographical area)?
- some or all of these?

These questions and their answers can be represented in a solutions table (see Planning Tool 2 opposite.

Planning Tool 2: Solutions Table

One aspect of assessing the situation involves managing and categorising the information that you have gathered. A simple Solutions Table can help you to do this.

Context

In mapping possible solutions, there are likely to be a wide range of different individuals, groups, and institutions who may have roles to play. It is likely too that different problems, and different ways of dealing with these problems, will be apparent at local, national, regional, and international levels.

Purpose

A Solutions Table is simply a tool for storing and summarising complex information in a format which should make it easier to manage and to present the information to others. This should help you to decide at which levels and in which arenas it is most appropriate for you to be active.

Method

1 At each of the geographic levels relevant to your work,
   - summarise the main problems, their causes and consequences;
   - describe the kinds of change that you want to see;
   - specify who needs to change in order for these changes to be achieved.

2 Summarise this information in the Solutions Table.

The Working Group for Weapons Reduction (WGWR) has gradually gained a better understanding of the problem of the proliferation and abuse of small arms in Cambodia. The group identified the following issues as the main obstacles to weapons-reduction efforts in that country.

Table 2.2: Solutions Table: obstacles to change in Cambodia

	At the local level	At the national level	At the regional and international levels
What are the problems and their causes and consequences?	The culture of violence is a legacy of decades of internal conflict. Although the fighting has ended, people continue to use weapons as the first solution to solve their problems. Even minor disputes often turn deadly. In local communities there is a serious lack of trust between civilians and the authorities responsible for maintaining security. Almost no dialogue takes place between civilians and local authorities on security and small-arms issues.	The creation of the National Commission for Weapons Reform and Management was a major step forward, but the Commission is not yet operational and it lacks the capacity, resources, and support needed to become effective.	Efforts by the government and the international community, supported by civil society, are now better resourced and timed, but they still lack a strong basis of understanding, and they are not comprehensive or well co-ordinated.
What kind of change do you want to see?	Dialogue needs to be encouraged between these groups to help to ensure that disarmament efforts are accepted, sustainable, and effective, and address underlying root problems.	Unless the attitudes of civilians, security forces, and authorities are modified, the demand for weapons will still remain. To transform this dependence on weapons into skills for non-violent conflict resolution is important work, requiring long-term commitment.	Without a strategy to develop capable, resourced, and self-led Cambodian efforts, current activities will be of limited effectiveness. An internationally supported long-term strategic plan is needed.
Who needs to change?	• security forces • local authorities • civil society/civilian groups	• Police, armed forces, and other security forces must develop new policies and practices. • Individuals and groups must find ways to deal with their own fears and find common solutions to improve security.	Regionally and internationally, institutional support for the government is needed, to increase its understanding and capacity to carry out the work.

Figure 2.6: Template for a Solutions Table

	At the local level	At the national level	At the regional and international levels
What are the problems and their causes and consequences?			
What kind of change do you want to see?			
Who needs to change?			

Analysing your environment

Thinking about your (internal) organisation and your (external) environment will help you to maximise your potential and avoid problems as you develop your plan.

Considering how to use your particular experience and other strengths in order to respond to the main features of the environment enables you to choose approaches that have the best chance of success.

Analysing your environment involves considering two elements:

- external factors: the main political, social, and economic conditions that might affect your ability to make a contribution
- internal factors: your strengths, experience, resources, and contacts.

External factors: key questions to address

The proliferation and misuse of small arms can have an enormous impact on political, social, and economic conditions. Arms proliferation is often used by states as a foreign-policy tool and is treated as an issue of national security. Even in countries where the State and civil society co-exist and co-operate, those in power may strongly resist the idea of discussing or providing information on small arms – let alone accepting civil society as a legitimate partner.

However, there will also be positive trends in society that are beneficial to your work, such as a government's desire to be regarded as a key international player which has put its own house in order.

All kinds of environmental factors will affect your work. To help you to identify the most important of them, consider the following questions. (Some sources of information which may help you to answer them are listed in Part 4.)

What political factors could have a critical influence on our work?

How do key institutions function?

For instance:

- Are government and State institutions accessible to members of the public and civil society?
- Do regional, national, and local governments have significant decentralised authority?
- How do the military and police operate?
- Is the judicial system impartial?
- How much influence do international donors have on government policy?
- Who else outside the country has influence?

- Which institutions are likely to present opportunities for our work, and which are likely to present obstacles?

What are the levels of public accountability?

For instance:

- Which groups have power, and which are excluded?
- How (if at all) is policy change monitored and enforced?
- Does corruption play a significant role in how decisions are taken? At what levels?
- Do decision makers behave in an open and transparent way? How do they communicate their decisions to the public, if at all?
- Do we have access to information about decisions made?
- What is the basis (if any) on which decision makers are held accountable?
- What ways (if any) exist for making sure that decision makers are accountable?
- What kind of access are we likely to get to decision makers?

What social factors might influence our work?

For instance:

- Are the media wholly State-controlled? Are they allowed to be critical?
- How will we be portrayed by the media?
- How strong is civil-society organisation? How independent?
- Is civil society permitted to participate in political life?
- How are we, as representatives of civil society, likely to be viewed by the decision makers whom we may wish to influence?
- Who is likely to support or oppose us?
- How are electronic communications used and viewed in society?

What economic factors might influence our work?

For instance:

- How much does a gun cost on the black market?
- How do small arms affect local and national economies? What are the economic benefits? What are the costs?
- How does conflict affect people's access to resources?
- How does the overall state of the economy affect our ability to operate?
- What relationship, if any, does the government have with donor countries?
- What economic alternatives are there?

Internal factors: key questions to address

Does our organisation have legitimacy?[2]

For instance:

- For whom does our organisation speak?
- Who will accept our right to speak out on the abuse of small arms?
- Who questions our legitimacy? Why ?
- How can we increase our legitimacy?

Does our organisation have credibility?

For instance:

- What ways do we use to communicate?
- How reliable is the information that our group provides to the public?
- Are our organisation's leaders seen as trustworthy and knowledgeable?
- How can we increase our credibility?

Is our organisation accountable?

For instance:

- Who makes decisions in our organisation or coalition?
- How open is the decision-making process?
- To whom are decision makers within the coalition accountable?
- How are they held accountable?
- How are members informed and involved?
- How do we communicate our progress to others outside the organisation?
- How can we improve our accountability?

Is our organisation prepared?

For instance:

- What past experience do we have that will be most relevant to the present situation?
- Do we have access to the research that we need to make our case convincingly?
- Have we considered and prepared for possible risks (physical, legal, etc.) to the security of our organisation?
- Have we considered and taken into account the gender-related aspects of our work?
- Have we identified the key stakeholders in the issue?
- What do we need to do to improve our preparedness?

For more on security and risk issues, see Section 2 in Part 3 of the Handbook. For more on research, see Section 3 in Part 3.

Is our organisation well placed to work with others?

For instance:

- What are our previous experiences of working with others?
- Which have been our best partnerships, and why?
- What can we learn from these experiences to ensure that future relationships are more successful?

For more on working with others, see Section 1 in Part 3.

Does our organisation have sufficient resources?

For instance:

- Do we have the physical resources that we need?
- Do we have the right people with the right experience and skills?
- Are our people and other resources deployed in the best way?
- How could we better match our resources and our programmes?

Does our organisation have secure funding?

For instance:

- Are there good systems of financial control within the organisation?
- Do we expect significant changes in our expenditure over the next two–three years?
- Can we predict how our sources of income will develop over the next two–three years?
- Are we getting money from a wide range of donors and funders?
- What are the financial priorities for our organisation, and do we have plans to meet them?
- What measures can we take to improve the security of funding?

For more on funding, see Section 4 in Part 3.

Planning Tool 3: SWOT Analysis

One aspect of assessing a situation involves analysing the environment. A SWOT analysis – assessing your organisation's strengths, weaknesses, opportunities, and threats – can be used to help you to do this.

Context

To be effective, usually it is vital to base your programme of work on a realistic assessment of what is possible and where your intervention is likely to be most successful. This depends to a large extent on being able to match your internal capacities with the external situation. See below for a good example of a SWOT analysis that was developed as a means of understanding a real situation, constructed by South Asian NGOs.

Purpose

Conducting a SWOT analysis can help you to develop an overall sense of the main factors – both internal and external – that will have an influence on your work. The format of the SWOT analysis should help you to identify, discuss, and manage some of the issues that face your organisation.

Method

A SWOT analysis organises information by breaking it down into the following categories:

- **strengths (internal)**: the positive aspects of your organisation;
- **weaknesses (internal)**: the factors within your organisation that might inhibit your work;
- **opportunities (external)**: the factors in society that could positively affect your work;
- **threats (external)**: the factors in society that could have a negative impact on your work.

Conducting a SWOT analysis involves identifying the major factors and issues affecting your work in each of these categories. You can do this either in a 10–15 minute exercise (using the Golden Rules of Brainstorming on page 67); or as a final activity, summarising a more detailed background analysis (based perhaps on the questions outlined in the section on analysing your environment, pp. 80–81).

Once you have captured the information, you should use it to consider the following:

- how you can counter or minimise your weaknesses and the threats you face;
- how you can maximise your strengths and exploit your opportunities.

Notes

Your SWOT analysis should prove to be a useful tool throughout your planning. You should find it helpful to refer to as you develop your plans; use it to check that the programme you are planning is realistic and makes sense, given the situation as it really is.

Example of a SWOT analysis: the South Asia Small Arms Network

The following is an abbreviated example of a SWOT analysis. It was produced by representatives of civil society across South Asia in February 2003 to identify the problems, challenges, and opportunities related to their work on the abuse of small arms in the region. The planning group used this tool during a meeting to identify priorities for regional action to be taken by the South Asia Small Arms Network. The group was keen to analyse the external environment, but to do so in the context of a detailed understanding of the range of skills, experiences, and resources that network members could contribute.

As in this example, a SWOT analysis sometimes produces generalities which could apply to many similar situations, and sometimes it produces more specific points that make it possible to make strategic choices about priorities.

Figure 2.7: SWOT analysis – South Asia Small Arms Network

Strengths (internal)

- Existing SASA-Net members and others
- Growing civil-society movement
- Women's groups are involved
- Good work on the UN Programme of Action on Small Arms and Light Weapons
- Passion and commitment of members
- Connection at the community level
- Other activist communities who can/should work on small arms and light weapons
- Work on small arms and light weapons provides the agenda for peace
- Some existing research – i.e. on legislation in South Asia
- International context/IANSA

Weaknesses (internal)

- Lack of strategy to push for changes in governance
- Network needs to expand
- Lack of precise and accurate research/data
- Need to engage young people
- Little dialogue between government and civil society
- Lack of human stories – need to highlight the personal impact
- Very limited resources
- Media not engaged by civil society
- No dialogue between civil-society stakeholders
- No campaign materials
- Lack of documentation on learning so far
- Lack of discipline and focus
- No common civil-society agenda in South Asia
- Lack of clear/simple messages

Opportunities (external)

- Anti-war in Iraq movement
- International organisations
- Peace process in Sri Lanka
- Interest from police in training
- Millions of civilians are opposed to the abuse of small arms
- Opportunity to mobilise against bad governance
- National commission in Sri Lanka
- People understand the issue as important
- Support from donors, including CIDA
- Some parts of South Asia Association for Regional Cooperation (SAARC) work – i.e. technical committees
- SAARC is doing monitoring work which is transferable
- War Against Terror
- Changing attitudes of some sections of the army
- Programme of Action
- Include non-violence in curriculum
- Connect SALW themes to other issues
- Afghanistan case study
- Focus on human rights and development as well as technical aspects
- People are tired of conflicts
- The time is right for action
- UN Review Conference
- Engage existing diplomacy efforts

Threats (external)

- Strength of the arms lobby
- Civil-society impact has weakened since September 11th 2001
- Civil society is not mobilised
- Weapons not collected
- Inadequate governance
- SAARC not functioning as well as hoped
- Public opinion not mobilised
- Macro problems of poverty and globalisation
- Threat to marginalised communities
- Non-cooperation by national governments
- Lack of commitment and political will
- Poor certification of weapons
- Lack of transparency on production
- Government legislation not implemented
- India/Pakistan conflict
- Increase in exports
- Easy availability of SALW
- Arming of ethnic groups
- Hypocrisy of supplier countries
- Media not engaged
- Lack of understanding of the UN Programme of Action – lack of clear messages
- The amount of money in the SALW market
- Deterioration of money in South Asia market
- Lack of DDR – Demobilisation, Disarmament, and Reintegration
- Impact on human rights
- Illicit production

HANDOUT

Figure 2.8: Template for a SWOT analysis

Strengths **What are the positive aspects within our organisation that could be important in our work?**	**Weaknesses** **What are the factors within our organisation that might inhibit our work?**
Opportunities **What are the factors in society (external to our organisation) that could positively affect our work?**	**Threats** **What are the factors in society (external to our organisation) that could have a negative impact on our work?**

Assessing the situation: summary and conclusion

In this section of the handbook we have argued that the first phase in designing, developing, and planning an effective programme of action requires time to be spent on an assessment of the situation in which one is working. Essentially this involves asking two fundamental questions:

- What are the problems that we face, and what are their possible solutions?
- What are the factors in our environment that may help or hinder our work?

This section introduced three tools designed to help you to focus and organise your analysis during this phase of planning:

- Problem and Solution Tree
- Solutions Table
- SWOT Analysis

Once you have a good understanding of the situation that you are in, you should be in a much better position to consider the changes that you can achieve. The next section suggests methods to help you to establish clear goals.

Phase 2: Establishing goals

Introduction

This phase involves the following steps:

- Prioritising solutions
- Setting goals

Having assessed the environment in which you plan to act, and having reached a clear and common judgement of the situation you are facing, you are in a much better position to identify and make clear what you are trying to achieve.

This phase in the process is important: it will enable you to use limited resources most effectively, for two reasons:

- Prioritising solutions is the first step towards making sure that what you seek to achieve is manageable, realistic, relevant to the context of the external environment, and commensurate with your own ability to respond to it.
- Being clear about your goal should give clarity to your whole programme of work, by sharpening the focus and helping you to think through how the change that you seek will actually happen.

Once you have considered these questions, you will be well placed to consider how you intend to achieve the goal that you have defined.

Prioritising solutions

If you have previously developed a Problem and Solution Tree (see Phase 1), you will probably have identified a number of different solutions that address the problems you are facing. However, given the limited availability of resources, you will probably want to focus your efforts on a specific solution, rather than trying to address everything.

Concentrating on a single solution can help you to achieve change and target your resources; but it can also distract attention from wider problems or deeper causes. Don't forget that your work on a specific issue should be a step towards the wider vision of a world free of the scourge of small arms, as expressed, for example, in the Nairobi Declaration (see page 51 of Part 1 of this manual).

Key questions to address

Using the answers to the following questions, you should be able to identify the most appropriate solution for your situation. You are then in a position to determine what you hope to achieve.

Think about this in the context of the external political, economic, and social environment and in terms of your organisational capacity. If you have conducted a SWOT analysis (see Planning Tool 3 in Phase 1), you have already developed an excellent understanding of the context in which you plan to act.

For each potential solution, consider the following questions.

What is the potential impact?

- How significant would be the impact on the lives of affected individuals and communities if the solution were adopted?
- Who would benefit and who would not?

What are the prospects of success?

- Is it realistic to assume that some kind of change will actually occur?
- Will we be able to maintain action throughout the timeframe of likely change?
- Is it likely that there could be changes that do not achieve our proposed solution but still would benefit affected individuals and communities?
- Who will oppose us, and how powerful will their opposition be?

What is the internal rationale for our organisation to work on this issue now?

- Does working on this issue fit with our organisational values, mission, and mandate?
- Does it play to our strengths and minimise our weaknesses?
- Do we have sufficient resources? How might it affect future funding?
- How might it affect important relationships?
- Do our efforts complement the programme of a wider movement?
- What additional benefits does our organisation bring by getting involved on this issue?

What is the external rationale for our organisation to work on this issue now?

- Does working on the issue respond to specific opportunities?
- Can we minimise the impact of any threats?
- What are the security implications? What other risks are there? Are they manageable?
- Does it help to link local and global concerns?
- Can we picture a sequence of achievable steps that will lead to our proposed solution?

Planning Tool 4: Ranking Solutions

A ranking exercise can help you to establish your goals (the second phase in the planning process).

Context

Although it is tempting to try to address all the problems that you face, in practice you are likely to be more successful and effective if you focus your efforts on achieving change in particular areas.

Purpose

Deciding where to focus your efforts is vital, and it is worth investing effort to make the right decision. A poor choice of focus at this stage can damage your ability to achieve change. One useful tool in helping you to make a decision is a ranking exercise. It enables you to make direct comparisons between various options against a standard set of key criteria.

Method

This ranking exercise is based on a simple scoring technique:

1 List the range of options that you have identified as possible solutions.

2 For each possible solution in turn, consider how well it scores against four criteria:

- potential impact
- prospects of success
- internal rationale
- external rationale

3 Give each solution a score between 1 and 5 against each criteria, where 1 is a very weak match, and 5 is a very strong match.

4 Add up the scores and use the totals as a basis for reaching a decision about where to focus your efforts.

Notes

You should base your assessments on earlier analysis that you have conducted (e.g. your SWOT analysis).

In making your final choice, use the total score as a guide to inform group discussion, in order to reach a consensus. If different solutions have similar scores, consider which criteria are the most important: for example, is the likelihood of success the most important consideration for the group, or is potential impact more crucial?

Building on their analysis of the problem and possible solutions (as summarised on page 74), Kosovan NGO FIQ considered each of the solutions and did a quick ranking exercise, scoring each of the potential solutions against the criteria, as described. This proved to be a helpful tool in developing FIQ's programme, because it was a simple and quick way of comparing the various available options.

Table 2.3: Ranking Solutions – FIQ, Kosovo

Possible solutions	Potential impact	Prospect of success	Internal rationale	External rationale	Total score
Training of journalists	4	4	5	5	18
Conducting survey	5	5	3	5	18
Public education	5	5	2	5	17
Building trust	5	4	4	5	18
Transparency: public information	5	1	2	5	13
Advocacy for legislation	3	4	4	3	14
Media events and round tables	5	5	4	5	19

Drawing on a combination of this exercise and earlier analysis of their external and internal situations, FIQ decided to focus their efforts on conducting a public survey to gauge people's attitudes to the problem of the proliferation of small arms.

Figure 2.9: Template for Ranking Solutions

Possible solutions	Potential impact	Prospect of success	Internal rationale	External rationale	TOTAL SCORE

Setting goals

Setting goals sounds deceptively simple. In practice, being clear about what you are trying to achieve can be the most difficult part of the whole planning process. It is also the most important. The clearer you can be about what you are trying to achieve, the easier it will be to identify the best ways of achieving it. If you are not clear about your goals, it will be difficult to communicate them to others.

Once you have decided which issue to work on, and have proposed the solution(s), you should decide on your goals. You can then keep reconsidering them, trying to make them more clear and more specific as your plans take shape.

Key questions to address

To set your goals, you need to ask two crucial questions:

What kind of change are we seeking?

You may find it helpful to review any earlier analysis that you conducted, examining the range of solutions to the problem (for instance by looking back at the earlier guidelines on mapping solutions).

At this stage you should aim to define the change in relation to one of the following:

- institutional policy
- institutional practice
- individuals' attitudes and opinions
- individuals' actions.

Who needs to change?

To answer this question, you need to identify the target. The target is the decision maker, the individual (or group) with the power to make the change that you are seeking. They may be one of the following, for example:

- the government minister responsible for the import and export of arms;
- a community leader or elder responsible for bringing security and stability to a local region;
- the head of the institution responsible for funding and implementing weapons-surrender programmes;
- the commissioner of police.

When setting your goal,

- Be as exact as possible. Specify which institution, what policy, which individuals, etc., need to change, and state as precisely as possible what kind of change is needed.

- Focus on the ultimate change that you are trying to achieve, the change that will have an impact on people's lives. It is very important to be clear about this. Do not focus on the means that you will adopt to achieve your end – for instance, the number of seminars you will organise, or the number of posters that you will produce – but focus on the end itself, the change that you want to see in the lives of those affected by the problems that you seek to address.

Getting this right is the foundation upon which your programme of action will be built.

Establishing goals: summary and conclusion

In this section of the handbook we have argued that, once you have assessed your situation, you are in a position to define your goals. Essentially this involves two steps:

- prioritising solutions so that you can focus your programme of action;
- clarifying the change that you are seeking, and identifying the people who need to change in order to achieve it.

This section introduced one tool designed to help you to focus and organise your analysis during this phase of planning:

- Ranking Solutions

Once you have defined your goals, you should be well placed to develop a strategy which helps you to make the most effective use of the opportunities available to you. The next section describes methods that may help you to think about means to make the change happen.

Phase 3: Developing a strategy

Introduction

This phase of the planning process consists of the following three steps:

- Framing the issue
- Identifying and categorising stakeholders
- Devising an influencing strategy

Once you have established your goal and considered its main implications – in particular through identifying who must change, and how – you can then think about the best ways to make this change happen.

This stage in the process is important in enabling you to use limited resources most effectively, for the following reasons:

- Unless you understand the forces for and against change, you may not be in a position to decide how best to act to obtain the change that you desire.
- It is an opportunity to think strategically about the best means available to you to influence your target. This will enable you to focus only on what is likely to be effective, and to avoid wasting time on approaches that have little chance of success.

Once you have considered these questions, you will have all the tools in place to be able to develop your plan of action.

Framing the issue

The experience of the International Campaign to Ban Landmines (ICBL) provides one very valuable lesson: that strong and clear messages are crucial to the success of campaigning and popular advocacy. When you are developing your campaigning plans, remember that a bold call for definitive standards, rather than looking for consensus and universal support, has been shown to be an important and successful way of engaging and motivating supporters.

Being very clear about what you want to change and what you want your audience to do to achieve the change is important as a means of communicating the purpose of your action. It also provides the imperative for the audience to take action.

In the case of the ICBL, the development of this strong message entailed a 're-framing' of the issue, turning the banning of landmines into a humanitarian objective, rather than a military issue about arms control. This re-framing provided a different focus to the issue and opened it up to new groups of potential supporters. Talking about the issue in terms of human suffering – 'the human cost of war' – also had the advantage of playing to the strengths of civil-society organisations (who understood the *realities* of that suffering) and the weaknesses of their opponents (who tended to be more focused on the *theory* of warfare).[3]

Planning Tool 5: Framing the Issue

Framing the issue can be an important and useful step in developing your strategy.

Context

Once you have established your goal, it is a good time to consider how you will communicate about the issues that you will be focusing on, to both internal and external audiences.

Purpose

A proposition statement that frames the issue can be used as a basis for building support for your work, both internally and externally. The process of developing the statement can be a good way of reaching consensus about the essential core of your work and communicating this to existing and potential supporters. A proposition statement is an encapsulation of the problem, your position, your proposed solution, and the action that you want taken.

Table 2.4: How to frame your issue

A short summary of the PROBLEM	A brief outline of your POSITION	Your suggested SOLUTION	The ACTION that you want to be taken
In stating the problem, you should try to focus on the core problem and describe how people are affected by the situation.	In other words, what is your response to the problem? Include an explanation of why you hold this view, if possible briefly referring to any research or other evidence that supports your thinking.	As outlined in the section on Setting Goals, your solution is likely to involve one or more of the following: • institutional policy change • changes in institutional practice • changes in individuals' attitudes and opinions • changes in the way that individuals act. Be as specific as possible.	In describing the action that you are calling for, you should try to identify all the relevant audiences and what you hope that each can contribute.

HANDOUT

Method

1 First, brainstorm some answers to the four central questions:

- What is the problem?
- What is your position?
- What is your solution?
- What is the action that you want to be taken?

If you have done some of the earlier exercises, you will already have covered much of this ground, so now you may simply to need to review and check your earlier thinking.

2 Next, for each column, amalgamate the results of the brainstorm, in order to reach agreement about the central message that you wish to communicate.

3 Finally, turn what you want to say into four sentences, one for each of the four columns. These sentences combined should frame your issue in one paragraph.

Notes

Being very clear about what you want to change and what you want your audience to do to achieve the change is very important in helping you to think about how best to proceed. It can also be surprisingly difficult: it may reveal previously unrealised differences of opinion among the participants.

HANDOUT

Figure 2.10: Template for framing an issue

What is the problem?	What is our position?	What is our solution?	What is the action that we want ?

Identifying stakeholders

All kinds of relationships will affect your work. There will be a variety of individuals and institutions, or 'stakeholders', whose interests include aspects of the problem of small arms that are relevant to your own priorities. The term *stakeholder* includes any individual or organisation who is either interested in or directly affected by the position that you take on a particular issue.

Work to end the abuse of small arms invariably involves a call for change. Some people, often very powerful, benefit from the current situation and may be opposed to any change. Your organisation, however well supported and effective, is sure to have limited resources, which will probably be much smaller than those of your opponents. Therefore it is crucial to identify the opponents of change and your potential allies.

If, for example, you aim to improve local community policing in the area where you live, you will need to work out who supports your position and who opposes it. You can do this by considering the attitudes of the people and groups who are interested in or affected by your position, such as local police officers, local government officials, victims of crime, and those who currently benefit from the *status quo*. It is beneficial too to consider the importance of the issue to them, as well as the influence that they wield.

Figure 2.11: Identifying stakeholders and finding out more about them

You need to research:	How to find out more
Which government departments are responsible for: • import and export of arms • negotiations and participating in international/regional forums • law enforcement and border controls • national defence and military policy • regulation of civilian possession of firearms • finance • development and grant making • provincial and local government	• Does your government produce a directory? • Does it have a website outlining what different departments do? • Are there other civil-society organisations working with governments who could give you the information? • Are UN agencies operating in your country or region (UNDP, UNICEF, Department of Peacekeeping Operations, etc.) from whom you could obtain information? • Can you get the information from local government or community leaders?
Which other organisations and individuals have a major interest in your issue? • NGOs • community groups • media • political parties • members of parliament • police • business • labour organisations • women's groups • youth groups • religious groups • academics • elders and community leaders • judiciary	• Ask IANSA (www.iansa.org) if other local NGOs are working on small-arms issues. • Have any political parties produced statements on small-arms abuse? • Are there public records of parliamentary debates, or is there public access to parliamentary sessions?
Which international players have an interest in your issue? • donors • NGOs • UN bodies • Regional groups (e.g. Organisation of American States, EU, etc.) • Transnational corporations involved in arms industry • Trade unions • International financial institutions • IANSA • Other governments that are working to introduce new policies on the proliferation of small arms	**Do any big international NGOs that work to counteract the abuse of small arms have country or regional offices close to where you work? Try** • Oxfam GB • World Council of Churches • Amnesty International • International Committee of the Red Cross/ Red Crescent. Contact the UN Department for Disarmament Affairs for access to reports and work on small arms within the UN system, plus statements, positions, and voting records of member states. (Contact details for these and many other organisations are given in Part 4 of this book.)

Categorising stakeholders

When identifying potential allies and opponents, it is first important to make sure that you have identified the widest possible group. To begin, take a blank piece of paper and have a brainstorm to name all stakeholders. At this stage, do not try to analyse them. Make sure that you name them explicitly: for example, 'business' will not help your analysis; instead, name actual companies with a direct interest in your issue, and state what they do. After this, you should try to focus on the most important stakeholders, through a process of categorisation.

Categorising stakeholders will help you to understand their current position on the issue. This will help you to decide how you might relate to them, now and in the future. One way to categorise stakeholders is to group them under the following four headings.

1 **The target:** Your target is the decision maker – the individual or group with the power to make the change that you are seeking. See below for advice on devising an influencing strategy.

2 **Beneficiaries:** These are the people whose lives you hope will be improved by the successful achievement of your goals. (See Phase 6 on evaluation for advice on how to assess the impact on beneficiaries.)

3 **Opponents:** Those who oppose what you are trying to do. Some could become allies in time, when they have understood the issues, or they could stand in the way of what you're trying to do, in which case they may become targets. Opponents may include, for example:

- the government department or minister responsible for the promotion of arms sales
- arms manufacturers
- armed criminal groups
- warlords or rebel leaders fighting for territory or access to resources
- non-State actors who have opted for the use of violence as a policy.

Identifying likely opponents: key questions to address

What are the blocks to change?

- what entrenched ideologies?
- what vested interests?
- what structural barriers?
- what social exclusions?
- what information restrictions?

Who benefits from the current situation?

- Who benefits economically (e.g. gun runners, manufacturers, etc.)?
- Who benefits politically (either within government, or others whose power depends on small arms)?
- Who is likely to actively oppose us?
- What motivates them to oppose us?
- How powerful are they?

4 **Allies:** People and organisations who support you because they share your values, or they will benefit either directly or indirectly from the changes that you are trying to bring about. They may include, for example:

- religious leaders
- community leaders
- sympathetic journalists
- politicians or political parties
- funders (see Section 4 on securing funding in Part 3 of the handbook).

Identifying likely allies: key questions to address

Who is losing from or disadvantaged by the current situation?

Who else might want to see the situation change?

How powerful are they?

Why should we work with them?

How could we work with them?

See Section 1 on working together in Part 3 of the handbook.

Planning Tool 6: Force-field analysis

A force-field analysis is a useful tool to help you to think about developing a strategy.

Context

You are not working in isolation. It is important to consider the other key players, or stakeholders, who have an interest in what you are doing, whose actions or attitudes may affect your ability to achieve change.

Purpose

A forcefield analysis can be a useful tool for understanding the power of your allies and opponents over the issue that is of concern to you. It is a good visual technique for representing the relative strengths of the supporters of change and the opponents who are likely to try to prevent that change from happening. It can form a basis for deciding the kinds of strategy that you will adopt to increase the pressure for change and minimise resistance. It is an important tool for helping you to identify where you might best focus your efforts to achieve these ends.

Method

Forces acting in two directions can be represented in terms of supporters for change and opponents resisting change.

1 Take a sheet of paper and, using the template provided below, briefly describe the current situation in the box in the middle of the page.

2 On a separate piece of paper, brainstorm a list of all the supporters of change.

3 Then consider each in turn, deciding on their relative importance.

4 Represent each force for change as an arrow. Each arrow should be labelled; the size of the arrows should represent the relative strengths of the various individual forces.

5 Once you have identified the forces for change, you may also identify potential assets that are not being put to use in support of change.

6 Now brainstorm a list of all those resisting change.

7 Then consider each in turn, deciding on their relative power/strength.

8 Represent each force for change as an arrow. Each arrow should be labelled; the size of the arrows should represent the relative strengths of the various individual forces.

The force-field shows that if the forces are equal, the situation will remain unchanged. To effect change, you must either increase the power of your allies, or neutralise or reduce the power and influence of your opponents.

Notes

You should base your assessments on analysis that you have previously conducted (for example, your SWOT analysis).

In many circumstances, it is easier to reduce the restraining force than to try to increase the supporting forces.

Example

Figure 2.12 represents an example of a force-field analysis constructed by representatives of civil society from across Eastern Africa in Nairobi, Kenya in November 2002, during a workshop exercise to identify ways forward in tackling some of the key small-arms issues affecting the region.

Figure 2.12: Potential allies and opponents of change in East Africa

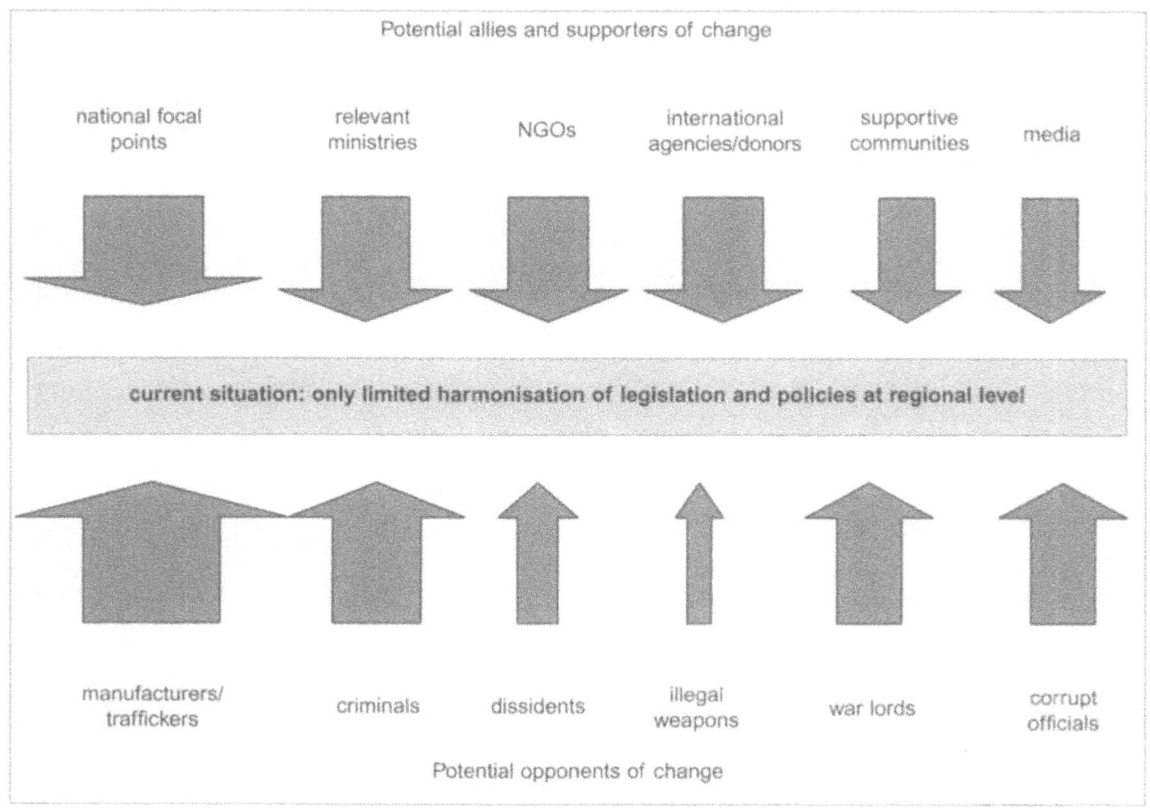

This analysis indicated to participants that the forces for change (the allies) had the potential to outweigh those opposed to it. However, they identified two major forces opposing change (manufacturers and criminals) whose influence had to be reduced to enhance chances of success. Similarly, several forces for change, including National Focal Points, NGOs, and international agencies, were identified as allies who needed to be supported to enhance their influence.

Figure 2.13: Template for a force-field analysis

Allies, potential allies, and forces for change (each represented as an arrow, with the size of the arrow indicating its relative importance)
Current situation
Opponents and restraining forces (each represented as an arrow, with the size of the arrow indicating its relative importance)

Devising an influencing strategy

Influencing your target – or decision maker – should be at the heart of your programme. As the force-field analysis shows, there will be many ways for you to exercise influence; sometimes you can do it directly, sometimes indirectly. Usually a combination of approaches works best. Your tactics should not operate as a series of isolated activities. That is why it is important to define your overall influencing strategy first.

Key questions to address

Who or what is the target?

The target is the decision maker – that is, the individual or group with the power to make the change that you are seeking. (You may have already addressed this question if you have considered the questions in Phase 2: Establishing Goals.) This is often much more difficult to determine than you might at first imagine – so make sure that you allow enough time to think this through carefully.

What is the target's current stance on the issue?

For political targets, consider the following:

- public statements and transcripts of speeches
- policy positions
- political ideology
- manifestos
- voting records on relevant issues
- response in debates
- response to your own correspondence.

If your target is a particular group:

- market research can be used to assess the current status of a certain group's knowledge, attitudes, and behaviours (and to track any changes over time);
- more informally, examples of what they say, write, or do should be gathered and recorded.

What would influence them on this issue?

As your own force-field analysis is likely to show, you may seek to influence the target directly, but there may be other, indirect routes that you could use in addition. These indirect routes are the channels of influence: the people and institutions that may influence the target on your behalf.

One way of building on your force-field analysis is to consider the forces for change in greater detail and prioritise the channels that you want to exploit. During the force-field analysis, it is likely that you have identified all the main routes (or channels) that are available to you to bring influence to bear on the decision maker; and those routes that you consider are likely to be the most influential (those with the biggest arrows).

To help you to decide which channels to prioritise, one additional question to consider is whether you have a good chance of persuading them to take action on your behalf.

A matrix of channels of influence can help you to analyse the range of routes available to you. It is based on an analysis of the quality of the two relationships involved in this influencing process – between you and the channel, and between the channel and the target.

When you have constructed a matrix, you will be able to draw up an influence map. This will help you to build up a picture of the routes that you will take to reach your decision maker.

Planning Tool 7: Matrix of Channels of Influence

A Channels of Influence Matrix can help you to develop your strategy.

Context

Having established your goal, you need to develop a strategy to achieve it. The most important element of this strategy will be identifying the means (or channels) that you will use to influence your target.

Purpose

In any situation, it is likely that there will be a range of channels open to you to influence your target. The trick is to identify the best ones, and then to focus your efforts on the most effective means available.

By considering the quality of the two relationships involved in this influencing process – between you and the channel and between the channel and the target – you will be able to make an appropriate selection of which channels to concentrate on.

Method

Using the template for a Channels of Influence Matrix:

1 Brainstorm a list of the channels of influence available to you.

2 Give each channel a score (high, medium, or low) to denote its likely effectiveness for influencing the target.

3 Give each channel a score (high, medium, or low) to denote your own likely effectiveness in influencing that channel.

4 Plot the results on the channels matrix.

5 Use these findings to prioritise channels and to develop tactics for achieving your goal.

Notes

Remember to think about informal influencing channels and opportunities as well as formal channels. For instance, is the President's wife interested in small-arms issues? Is the Police Chief likely to respond positively to a favourable opinion voiced by a close friend whom one of your members may know well?

Figure 2.14: Template for a channels of influence matrix

How effectively will you be able to influence the channel?

How much influence will the channel have with your target?		High	Medium	Low
	High			
	Med			
	Low			

Planning Tool 8: Influence Map

This technique complements and develops the previous tool: the Channels of Influence Matrix. It will help you to devise your influencing strategy.

Context

An Influence Map gives shape to your strategy and establishes the framework for your plan of action.

Purpose

An Influence Map is a tool that you might use in developing, presenting, and explaining your influencing strategy. It provides a simple visual guide to the routes that you will be taking in order to influence your target.

Method

Starting with a blank sheet of paper:

1 Place the target at the centre.
2 Around the target, write the main channels of influence that you will be using.
3 Identify any secondary channels that you plan to use. These are people or groups of people who can influence your main channels.
4 Use arrows to represent the influencing relationships.

See the example below.

Example: The Slovak NGOs Working Group

The Slovak NGOs Working Group on arms aims to increase the transparency of arms-trade issues and to strengthen the case for the introduction of greater parliamentary scrutiny of the national arms-export control system in the Slovak Republic, in line with EU standards. One aspect of this work has been to seek to persuade the Slovak government to publish an official Annual Report on Strategic Export Controls.

To achieve this goal, the Working Group's strategy of influence has been to focus on six priority channels:

- NGO representatives
- independent specialists and academics from research institutes
- parliamentarians
- the media
- government officials
- defence-industry representatives.

These are the primary channels, because they can exert influence directly on the target.

In addition, there will be secondary channels who can bring influence to bear, indirectly, through others. These secondary channels may be in a good position to influence the primary channels to advocate on their behalf. Often, as in this case, the same influence routes can be used in different ways. For example, the media might be a primary channel, directly influencing the government. But they are also a secondary channel to influence others, such as parliamentarians and defence-industry representatives, to raise the issue directly with the relevant minister.

Figure 2.15 is a simplified representation of the routes of influence identified during the Slovak campaign. For a more detailed explanation of the strategy developed by the Slovak NGOs Working Group, see the case study on pp. 120–121.

Figure 2.15: An influence map produced by the Slovak NGOs Working Group

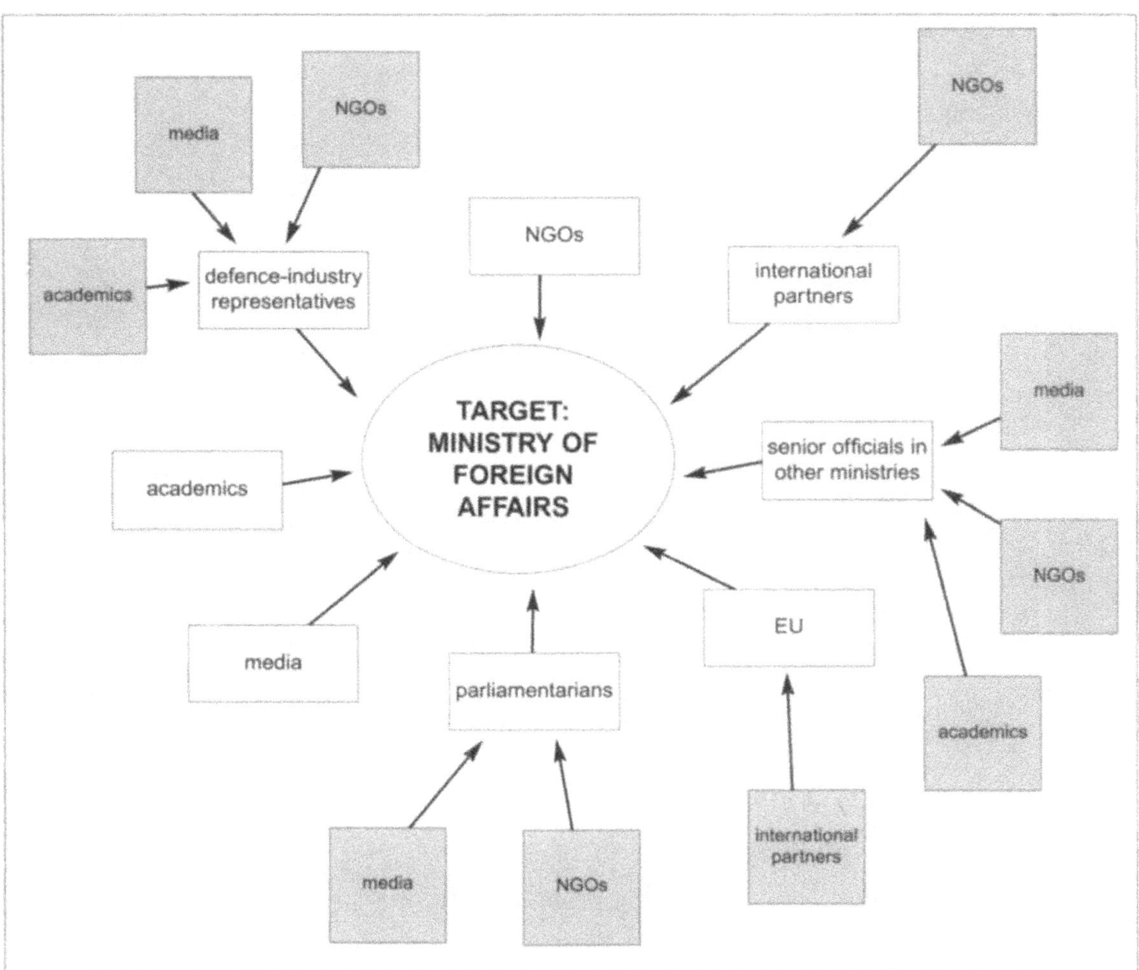

Developing a strategy: summary and conclusion

In this section of the handbook we have argued that, having established your goal, you should consider the best ways to achieve the desired change(s). Essentially this involves:

- understanding and assessing the supporters and opponents of change;
- considering ways of influencing the target, and selecting those that are likely to be most effective.

This section introduced four tools designed to help you to focus and organise your analysis during this phase of planning:

- Framing the Issue
- Force-field Analysis
- Matrix of Channels of Influence
- Influence Map

Once you have developed your influencing strategy, you are well placed to create your action plan.

Phase 4: Planning the activity

Introduction

This phase of the planning process involves the following steps:

- Setting objectives
- Developing an action plan

Having identified the means by which you can best influence your target, you need to decide on the details of your action plan. This phase in the process will enable you to use limited resources most effectively in the following ways.

- Setting clear objectives will lay out the steps between where you are now and where you want to be in the future, helping you to plot a clear pathway to your goal.
- Thinking through the actions that you will undertake helps you to determine how activities, resources, and objectives fit together.
- Action planning gives you a final chance to review whether you have been realistic in your assessment of what is possible.
- A detailed plan helps everyone involved to be clear about what they should do, in what time-frame, and why.
- Objectives and plans give you something against which to measure your progress, so that if you are heading in the wrong direction it will be obvious before it is too late.

Once you have planned your actions, you will be ready to implement your plan.

Setting objectives

Having established your influencing strategy, you will need to plan your approach in greater detail. At this stage, the clearer you can be about your objectives, the easier it will be for you to focus all your resources and energy on achieving them. Planning can be time-consuming, but good planning will prevent you wasting time later; it will give you a clearer purpose and a well-developed scheme of activities for achieving it. Planning helps you to clarify whom to target, when, and how. You will be in control of events and better prepared for action, and your activities will be more coherent and co-ordinated.

Key questions to address

You should have already established your goal (see Phase 2). A vital part of the planning process is to set (short-term) objectives which identify some of the steps on the way to achieving your ultimate (long-term) goal.

Achieving effective change on small-arms abuse is often a long-term process, so it is important to quantify your progress. Setting short-term objectives should help to maintain your motivation and demonstrate to your supporters and funders that your work is making progress.

Are we clear about the pathway to change?

You need to understand how individual elements of the situation fit together.

- How will changes in institutions lead to an improvement in the lives of affected individuals and communities?
- What degree of influence does the public have on key institutions?
- How far are you able to effect changes among the public?

Changes in institutions: Meaningful change occurs in institutions when there are changes in *institutional policy* and *institutional practice.* In most cases, policy-change is a means to an end. The subsequent changes in institutional practice are the key factors that lead to improved conditions for affected communities and individuals. In other words, a changed policy benefits people only if the policy is actually applied.

Organisations advocating change often concentrate on getting policy changed, but then they fail to monitor the change to make sure that it is being enforced. However, there often remains a gap between stated policy and actual practice, for a number of reasons, such as a lack of political will (because of competing priorities or corruption, for example), or a lack of institutional capacity to implement the new policy (because of limited resources or weak systems). Or the new policy is implemented in ways that were not expected when the policy was drawn up.

In addition, policy reform can be altered or reversed at any time. For example, in West Africa, the ECOWAS moratorium (see page 52 for details) contained many practical measures to curb the proliferation and misuse of small arms in the region. However, the actual benefits of the moratorium have so far proved limited, because change in policy has not led to changes in the behaviour of certain key governments. This is also the case with several international non-binding agreements. Strong organisation at both national and grassroots levels is likely to be needed in order to put pressure on governments and other authorities, and to push for greater access to information and greater levels of political accountability.

Changes among public groups: Meaningful change among individuals and groups occurs when there are changes in *attitudes* and *behaviour*. Changing people's attitudes and behaviour is not simple. Giving people new knowledge about an issue will not automatically lead them to change their attitudes (although it may be one of the contributing factors). Likewise, the development of new attitudes or beliefs will not automatically lead to changes in behaviour (although it is probably a vital stage in the process of behaviour change).

Public-change objectives may be focused either on individuals or on groups of individuals. For example, you could target police officers, or men who exhibit certain types of behaviour, or members of parliament. You should define these groups as precisely as possible.

The influence of the public on institutions: In some cases, institutions may change their policies and practices as a result of public action or public opinion on an issue. However, in some cases, what tends to influence political élites is the attitude and influence of other élites, not the opinion of the general public. It may make more sense to focus on the most important institutions, rather than seeking to raise awareness among – or influence the behaviour of – public audiences.

How will we know whether we are making progress towards our goal?

Objectives are intermediate steps that you need to take on the way to your ultimate goal. They provide a means for measuring progress, so that you know that you are moving towards your goal – or that you are not making progress, and you need to do something about it. When you set objectives, it is important to state them in such a way that you will be able to measure whether you have achieved them or not. And they should be stated as results – in other words in terms of real change, not just things that you plan to do.

This means setting objectives that are *specific* and *timetabled*. You should state as precisely as possible what you seek to change, and indicate a date by when you hope to achieve it.

Your objectives need to be informed by your analysis of the types of approach that will work. They should be derived from your previous assessment of the external environment and the internal realities of your situation. (SWOT analysis, stakeholder analysis, and force-field analysis are three useful tools for this task.) Your objectives should be *realistic* steps which lead to concrete change that will contribute to achieving your ultimate goal.

Once you have stated your objective in this way, you should reflect on whether it is actually *achievable* in the terms that you have suggested.

The following case study demonstrates how the Slovak NGO Working Group developed objectives as the focus for their action, and how they linked the formulation of their objectives with their detailed action planning.

Pathways to change: Slovak NGO Working Group

During the 1990s, weak export controls encouraged numerous irresponsible government-licensed arms transfers from Central and Eastern Europe. Today, transparency in the arms trade and controls on arms exports are a matter of concern not only because without them human rights are abused and development is undermined, but also because they are a requirement for membership of the European Union.

Although Slovakia, aspiring to membership of the EU, has already officially supported the EU Code of Conduct on Arms Exports, it has not so far taken any practical steps to implement its provisions. In Slovakia, official data relating to the production, holding, and export of arms are still very limited. There are no official government reports on arms exports, and no mechanisms in place for parliamentary scrutiny and government accountability. A culture of State secrecy is still deeply rooted in Slovakia – especially on matters of security – and, under current law, commercial arms-trade information is classified as a State secret.

The Slovak NGO Working Group has ambitions to change this situation and persuade the government to publish an official Annual Report on Arms Exports. It believes that increased transparency and parliamentary accountability will lead to strengthened national and regional controls on arms exports.

To achieve this goal, the Working Group's strategy of influence is to work through six channels: NGO representatives; independent specialists and academics from research institutes; parliamentarians; the media; government officials; and defence-industry representatives.

The Working Group identified seven steps along the pathway to achieving the final goal. These were outlined as follows:

1 Identify all governmental representatives working in the field of arms-export controls.
2 Strengthen NGO involvement in the monitoring of these issues.
3 Improve co-operation between NGOs and government bodies responsible for arms-trade issues.
4 Convince parliamentarians and the media of the need to take an active interest in monitoring arms-trade issues.
5 Organise an NGO round-table and an experts' round-table, together with appropriate media work.
6 Publish the first independent annual report on Slovak arms exports and present the findings to parliamentarians, the public, and the media.
7 Persuade the Slovak government to publish an official Annual Report on Strategic Export Controls, and discuss with it the scope and content of such a report.

These objectives have formed the basis for planning more detailed activities. Monitoring against these objectives continues, based on the following means of verification:

- consultations with project partners;
- interviews with government and civil servants at the beginning and end of the project, to track the changes in attitudes, beliefs, and behaviour;
- tracking the changes over time in the language of official letters and other responses from government;
- identifying the type and amount of information supplied by government civil servants following the change in legislation.

Progress to date includes the following:

- The creation of an arms-trade database, cataloguing contact details of government officials, MPs, advisers, 'umbrella' defence-industry organisations, producers, export companies, NGOs, and journalists. (This relates to Objective 1, above.)
- A growth in the number of groups and individuals working on arms-trade issues in Slovakia, and a strengthening of the cohesion of the Working Group. (Objective 2)
- Increasing media awareness of arms-trade issues through establishing contacts with selected journalists and exchanging information; creating an image of the group as consisting of independent experts on arms-trade issues, who are now contacted not only by journalists but also by everybody else who would like to discuss or confirm information and data related to this field. (Objectives 3 and 4)
- Three annual NGO/government round-table meetings have been organised, attended by governmental officials and defence-industry representatives, which help to create the conditions for further exchanges of information, knowledge, and experiences. The organisers reported that these round-table meetings were the most effective of all the instruments for achieving progress, providing a major channel for lobbying. (Objective 5)
- The first Independent Report on Slovak Arms Exports was presented to an expert audience of NGOs and journalists, attracting media and public interest in Slovakia and abroad. (Objective 6)
- Government officials have declared their readiness to publish an Annual Report, following a change in the legislation on secrecy matters. For this reason Parliament has been identified as the most important target institution for the next phase of the campaign. (Objective 7)

Developing an action plan

All action planning depends on local circumstances. However, such a plan always involves matching resources with objectives and with projected activities. Your activities are the means by which you will achieve the change identified in your objectives. Ensuring that you identify the most appropriate and effective action to achieve your objectives is fundamental to the success of your work.

Key questions to address

What activities will we undertake? What resources do we need?

Consider these two questions together in your action planning. To achieve each objective that you have set yourself, you should state what tasks need to be done, and in what sequence they need to be done. Then for each task, answer these questions:

- Who is responsible for getting it done?
- By when does it need to be done?

As when setting your objectives, you will need to build your action plan around the available opportunities for influencing people, institutions, or events. To remind yourself of the opportunities that you have previously identified, check the SWOT analysis that you conducted during earlier phases of your planning. (See pp. 84–87 for further information on conducting a SWOT analysis.)

Remember that your resources include staff time, and appropriate skills and competencies, as well as funding and other financial resources. In answering these questions, you should be realistic about your own capacity. If you do not have the resources that are adequate for the task that you are setting yourself, you need to identify how you will get extra resources: activities to achieve this then need to be included in your action plan. Remember to draw on all the strengths of your network or wider group of allies to fill any resource gaps that you identify. The alternative is to decide on a less ambitious set of objectives. Remember that at all stages in planning you should review where you have got to and, if necessary, amend your objectives.

An excellent way to organise your action planning is to produce a Gantt chart. See Planning Tool 9 on page 124for details of how to do this, with an example of a chart created by the Serbia and Montenegro Red Cross.

Have you anticipated changes in circumstances?

You are liable to encounter both obstacles and opportunities. As an organisation, you need to be adaptable enough to respond to events as they occur. Even the best plan can become irrelevant very quickly, if the situation changes. As far as possible, your planning should prepare you for this. Ensure that your plan is flexible by building in consideration of contingencies, so that you can adapt to changing circumstances as they arise. So-called contingency planning involves asking the following questions:

- How might the political environment change? How would this affect our work? How would we react if it happened?
- How might those whom we are targeting, and others, respond to our actions? How might this affect our subsequent activity? Have we taken this into account in our planning?

Look at the issue from every angle. Think about what might go wrong, or what might go better than you expect. Get others to test your plan. Think about external events and deadlines and how they might affect you. And keep planning, reviewing, and revising as circumstances change. Above all, bear in mind that the plan is just a tool to help you to reach the goal: if a really important opportunity arises unexpectedly, you will probably want to seize it, even if it delays your planned activities.

Planning Tool 9: Timelines – Gantt Chart

A Gantt Chart is a horizontal bar chart, developed as a production-control tool by Henry Gantt, an engineer. For a practical application, see the example of project planning by the Serbia and Montenegro Red Cross below.

Context

A Gantt chart pulls together the various elements of your plan and makes it clear who should be doing what, and when.

Purpose

Gantt charts have many uses. They provide a good way of displaying your action plan. They make your plan clear, so that all those involved share an understanding of what needs to be done, and they know when specific actions have to be completed, to ensure timely project delivery.

Such a chart lists the activities in an easy-to-read timeline, and it can help to reveal the relationships and the dependencies between activities. It is also a practical way to ensure that resources are not too thinly allocated at any one time.

Gantt charts are useful for sharing information about the plan, and they can be used as a basis for monitoring and reporting on progress.

Method

For each channel, or area of work:

1. List all the activities that you need to undertake. (Writing them on sticky Post-It notes may make it easier to arrange them.)
2. Arrange them roughly in the order in which they should happen.
3. Identify the likely duration of each activity.
4. Transpose this information on to the Gantt timetable (using the template).
5. Ensure that your activities are linked to any relevant external events or deadlines.

6 Ensure that the plan is synchronised – in other words that in all cases the things that need to happen in advance of a particular task have happened.

7 Ensure that you have adequate resources available to do all the work; if this is a problem, consider delaying or rescheduling some of the tasks.

8 When the chart is complete, allocate responsibility to named individuals for the completion of specific activities.

Notes

Gantt charts and similar forms of project planning are available as computer software; they can be very useful in this form, if you have access to a computer.

Example

In September 2001, the Serbia and Montenegro Red Cross launched a Small Arms Campaign to challenge and change public attitudes towards the proliferation and misuse of small arms. Figure 2.16 summarises some of the key steps that led to the launch.

Figure 2.16: Timeline for the launch of a small-arms campaign by the Serbia and Montenegro Red Cross

	Feb	Mar	Apr	May	Jun	Jul	Aug	Sep
1. PREPARATORY PHASE								
appoint co-ordinators	■							
seminar for co-ordinators	■							
data collection and research		■	■					
seminar for disseminators		■	■					
define target groups		■	■					
translate publication		■	■					
equip the centres		■	■					
prepare materials			■					
2. ACTIVITIES WITHIN THE SERBIA AND MONTENEGRO RED CROSS								
workshops for local branches			■	■	■			
discussion with government and NGOs			■	■	■			
discussion with media			■	■	■			
discussion with opinion leaders			■	■	■			
evaluate the campaign so far						■	■	
analyse the plan for the next phase						■	■	
3. PUBLIC CAMPAIGN								
launch the public campaign							■	

- **Preparatory phase:** The small-arms campaign was a new activity for the Serbia and Montenegro Red Cross. Owing to that – and because of the sensitive nature of the issues – it was necessary to prepare carefully for the campaign. It was decided to use existing structures, adapted to the needs of the campaign.
- **Activities within the Serbia and Montenegro Red Cross:** The first and most important task within this phase was to spread awareness about the campaign, in order to mobilise Red Cross people for working on it. In addition, in this phase it was planned to identify possible partners and provide support for appropriate government bodies.
- **Public campaign:** The campaign was planned to start in September with a launch, followed by a slow acceleration, gradually introducing new activities and means of publicising the initiative.

Figure 2.17: Template for a planning chart

Name of project: ____________________

time — divided into days/weeks/months →

Area or phase of activity 1 action 1								
action 2								
etc.								
Area or phase of activity 2 action 1								
action 2								
Etc								
Area or phase of activity 3								
Etc								

Planning activity: summary and conclusion

In this section of the handbook we have shown how, having identified the best ways of influencing your target, you should develop a more detailed plan of action. Essentially this involves

- plotting a pathway to your goal
- identifying how activities, resources, and objectives fit together.

This section introduced one tool designed to help you to focus and order your analysis during this phase of planning:

- the Gantt Timeline

Once you have produced your plan, it is time to implement it.

Phase 5: Implementation and monitoring

Introduction

As you implement your plan, you should always monitor your progress. This phase in the process is important because it helps you to identify what is working and what is not working. It also helps you to learn and to be adaptable, modifying your strategy and tactics as events develop.

As you find out more about the context in which you are operating, and as the situation changes, you should be prepared to revise the objectives that you established earlier. Effective monitoring, which involves comparing actual progress against objectives, should help you to do this appropriately. It may also be important for you to monitor the actions of others, so that you can identify and comment on their successes and failures, and above all learn from them. To do this, you need to gather information about the following:

- what you – or others – have been doing;
- the results achieved in key areas as a result of these interventions;
- the environment and the way in which it is changing, as a result of your interventions or for other reasons.

Developing a framework for monitoring

Key questions to address

What indicators will you use to monitor your progress?

Whether you are monitoring or evaluating your own work, or attempting to assess the effects of the work of others, you will need to state clearly what kinds of evidence you will consider in order to determine progress. These are your indicators.

Remember that an *objective* is a successful result: an *indicator* is some form of evidence which will measure progress (or lack of it) towards achieving that objective. Don't set arbitrary targets for your indicators (such as 'a 30 per cent fall in violent crime'). Often a direction of change will be enough ('a continuous fall in violent crime'). See Planning Tool 10 on page 131 for information on how to set indicators and their means of verification.

If you are assessing your own work, the indicators that you establish will relate to the objectives that you originally set (see Phase 4: Planning the Activity). When assessing the intervention of others, you may wish to use their own criteria, or relate their work to those things that you consider important.

What means of verification will help you to measure progress?

In most cases you will need to compile a range of evidence from a number of different sources. These sources of information that you will use to track your indicators are called the *means of verification.*

How will you report on your progress to stakeholders?

You should not forget that there will be a number of stakeholders who would benefit from knowing how your programme of work is progressing. Their opinions will also help you to judge if you are making progress. Being able to demonstrate success to those who support you or to those whom you are trying to influence is extremely important, so you should take time to ensure that this is done regularly. This group could include, for example:

- the individuals and communities whose lives you hope will be improved by your intervention
- project funders
- partners and allies
- policy researchers
- other civil-society organisations or governments interested in your work.

Each of these groups will have its own distinct communication needs, so when planning your schedule of work you should allow space and time for communication with them.

How will you use the information that you gather in order to amend your programme of action?

When your monitoring shows that your progress is diverging from the objectives that you have set, you have three basic choices:

- Change your work in order to refocus your efforts on achieving your objectives (if, for example, something you have been doing has not proved to be as successful as you had hoped). What you learn should give you good ideas for alternative strategies.
- Revise your objectives (if, for example, it is obvious that for some reason the original objectives are no longer realistic, or no longer relevant).
- Continue without change (if, for example, you judge that any difference is not a serious one).

As you measure your progress, make sure too that you take the time to celebrate and enjoy your successes.

For more advice on research techniques, see 'Gathering information through research' in Part 3 of the Handbook.

Planning Tool 10: Setting Indicators

Setting indicators is vital for monitoring progress.

Context

You should establish monitoring systems at the beginning of the project. This will allow you to make periodic judgements about your progress and adjust your work accordingly. From the outset, you should clarify what you are going to measure and then decide on the means of gathering the information that you need.

Purpose

Indicators are your measures of progress: tools for you to monitor your programme of action. Indicators must relate to the objectives that you have set. The task of monitoring progress can become very time-consuming, and there is a danger of wasting time in monitoring the wrong things. The tool presented here is useful because it makes explicit the links between your objectives and the indicators and means of verification that you will use.

Method

Using the template for setting indicators, consider the following questions in relation to each of your objectives.

1 What are the important pieces of evidence that will show whether this objective is being met, or not? These are your indicators.
2 How you might gather this information: what are the main sources and techniques that you will use? These are your means of verification.
3 Include the gathering of this evidence and the reviewing of progress in your plan.

Figure 2.18: Indicators set by Viva Rio

Project goal: a substantial improvement in the quality of life and a change in the general perception of danger by those who live and move through the cities of the State.

Objectives	**Indicators (measures of progress)**	**Means of verification (sources of information used to assess progress)**
1 Re-registering available firearms in the State of Rio de Janeiro. 2 Voluntary surrender of 30,000 firearms. 3 Apprehension of 40,000 illegal arms. 4 Application of existing law to control the illegal carrying of firearms. 5 Introduction of a new law to restrict the commercial arms trade.	Reductions in the following: • homicide rate • rate of gun-related injuries • number of firearms in circulation • use of arms • number of police injured and killed • number of civilians injured and killed by the police • number of incidents involving the use of arms in domestic and public spaces	These indicators then formed the basis for monitoring and evaluating the progress of the project. The methods included collecting both qualitative and quantitative data from the following sources: • Police, hospital, and coroners' reports – before, during, and after the campaign. • Police reports of the use of arms in robbery, domestic violence, drug-related crime, etc. • Police statistics on the numbers of arrests made for illegal possession of a firearm. • Numbers of civilians wounded or killed in confrontations with the police. • Qualitative and quantitative assessments of police efforts to retrain officers involved in firearms incidents. • Monitoring police efforts to devise new strategies to minimise the use of firearms. • Monitoring police use of ammunition. • Interviews with focus groups representing specific segments of the public to assess perceptions – e.g. youth, residents of shanty towns, middle-class professionals, gun owners, community leaders, law-enforcement officials. • Media coverage of the campaign. • Monitoring the numbers of arms exchanged and firearms re-registered. • Interviews with participants in arms-exchange and firearm-registration campaigns to assess their motivation to take part . • Ethnographic observation. • Quantitative monitoring of victim-assistance programme (numbers and types of assistance provided). • Qualitative assessment of the impact on victims and their families.

Figure 2.19: Template for setting indicators

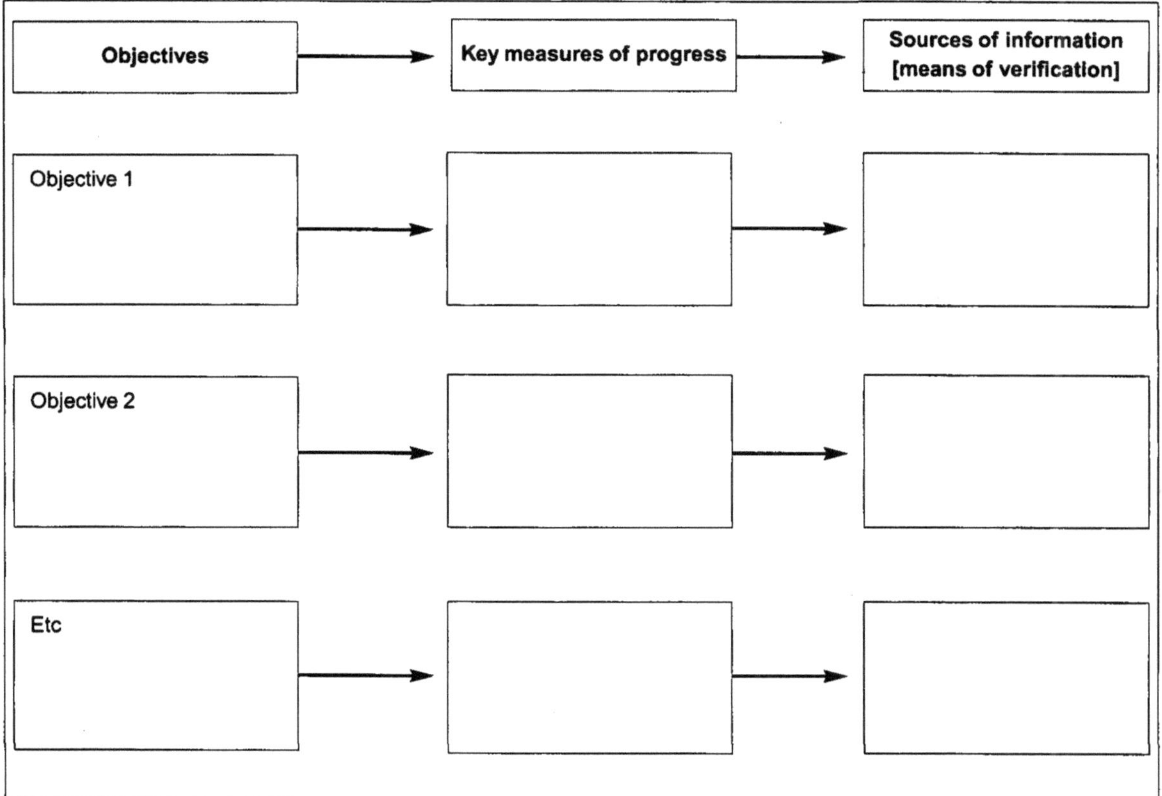

Implementation and monitoring: summary and conclusion

In this section of the handbook we have argued that, as you implement your plan, you should always monitor your progress. Essentially this involves the following steps:

- gathering information about what have been doing and how the external environment is changing – as a result of your interventions or for other reasons;
- identifying what is working and what is not working; changing strategy and tactics as events develop.

This section introduced one tool designed to help you to focus and organise your analysis during this phase of planning:

- Setting Indicators

Phase 6: Evaluation

Introduction

You should continually evaluate your programme, using the evidence that you gather from your monitoring systems. It is also important to conduct a more formal and structured evaluation at the conclusion of the programme.

This phase in the process is important in enabling you to use limited resources most effectively, for the following reasons:

- It allows you to look back and make judgements about past effectiveness (information which might be of interest to stakeholders such as funders).
- It allows you to learn from experience to improve future practice.
- It helps you to understand whether your actions have been as efficient as possible in utilising your resources to create change.

An important concept in evaluation is *impact assessment*. An impact assessment considers the links between the action that you take and any resulting changes in people's lives.

It is very difficult to prove without doubt that your programme of action has directly resulted in specific political and social changes. It is even more problematic to establish links between your programme of action and the impact on beneficiaries. This is because you are operating in a complex environment in which your own interventions don't take place in isolation from the activities of others, from the local context, or from the economic and political situation in which you are working.

What you can realistically aim to do, however, is to develop a reasonable argument to demonstrate whether your work has contributed to change. You can do this by gathering a range of evidence. Individual pieces of evidence, viewed separately, may not seem significant; but it is sometimes possible to draw reasoned conclusions from a critical mass of evidence by using a range of information sources, both qualitative and quantitative.

Tools for evaluation

Key questions to address

When you evaluate your work, you should gather the widest possible range of opinions. From these various perspectives, you can build up an overall picture of the contribution that you have made. All measures are affected by some degree of subjectivity. You need to be constantly aware of this as you design and implement your evaluation programmes, even being prepared to challenge the underlying assumptions of the approach that you take.

Where possible, you should set up monitoring systems so that you can cross-check your findings. To do this, you should involve people with a range of skills, experience, and points of view; and try to ensure that information about the same thing is collected in different ways from at least three sources, to ensure that it is reliable.

In designing your evaluation, you should consider the following questions:

Who should participate in the evaluation? How? On what terms? When?

If you want to assess changes in people's lives, it is essential to take account of the opinions and judgements of the intended beneficiaries. To do so adequately, you need to recognise and plan for diversity: allow for factors such as gender, class, ethnicity, religion, disability, and age, all of which tend to affect people's status, perceptions, values, and priorities.

Many evaluations take as their starting point the idea that affected communities are best placed to analyse their own situations and decide how the information is used, rather than for this to be done by external evaluators. Your evaluation activities should be performed in partnership with community members. Your plans and methods should be flexible, and you should be willing to review your findings continually, to decide how best to continue.

It is important too to try to evaluate how your work has affected people at different levels (individual, family, community, region, etc.). This helps you to develop a more coherent picture of what has changed, who has benefited, who has not benefited, and why.[4]

Think about the participation of the following audiences in the evaluation process:

- beneficiaries: those whose lives will be improved if you achieve your goals
- local community organisations and groups

- those who have been working on the issue within (and in partnership with) your organisation
- decision makers and government officials
- journalists and academics
- wider public audiences
- donors
- non-stakeholders (i.e. people who have not been involved in the work you are assessing) acting as a control group (against which to measure what has changed because of your work rather than because of other developments that would have led to the changes anyway).

Who will conduct the evaluation?

- Will you use internal and/or external evaluators?
- How can affected communities be involved in helping to analyse their own situations?

When should the evaluation be conducted?

In addition to evaluating your programme on completion, you may wish to set markers throughout its progress. Your evaluation process could, for example, include the following:

Periodic partner reviews	To review relationships, procedures, and progress against targets and agree contingency action as necessary.
Mid-term review	To review progress towards goals and to reassess the programme's strategic direction at the halfway point in its implementation.
Completion report	To identify what went well and what did not go well, as a basis for establishing and disseminating lessons learned.

Against what outcomes should the evaluation be conducted?

You should evaluate your programme against the objectives that you have set: have your objectives changed as your work has progressed? You should also evaluate against specific indicators that you may have identified in order to quantify the change that you desire.

Using what methods?

- How can you ensure that you are hearing from a range of voices and seeing things from a range of perspectives?

- How will you ensure that you gather sufficient data and information to make a reasonable judgement of the difference that your intervention has made?

See comments in section 3, 'Gathering information through research', in Part 3 of the Handbook, for some ideas of the various methods you could use.

How will findings and lessons learned be disseminated?

- Who needs to know the results of the evaluation?
- How and when will you share the information with them?

How will recommendations be followed up?

- What systems do you have in place within your own organisation to learn from evaluations and other reviews?
- Can you identify specific actionable recommendations: particular things that you and your organisation will do differently as a result?
- How will you encourage others to think about the implications for their work?

Evaluation of processes: questions to address

A process evaluation reviews the mechanics of a project. At its simplest level, this can be achieved by asking the following questions:[5]

- Has work been well organised and well communicated?
- Did your techniques function properly?
- Were the people whom you reached the ones whom you were seeking to influence?
- Were the selected targets and channels the appropriate ones?

Evaluations: summary and conclusion

In this section of the handbook we have argued that at certain times it will be appropriate to conduct a more formal and structured evaluation of your progress. Essentially this involves:

- looking back to make judgements about past effectiveness
- looking forward to improve future practice.

Tools and approaches to use in evaluation are explored in the research section in Part 3 of the handbook.

Part 3

Taking action

Contents

Introduction

Part 3 of the handbook introduces some basic advocacy techniques, with suggested sources of further information. It is based on the idea that, although the contexts may be very different in – for example – Manila and Madrid, the practice of advocacy derives from some core principles which are potentially useful to all activists, wherever they are working.

The details of any advocacy programme will of course be different in every case and in every situation. You will need to adapt the suggested approaches to your own circumstances. This part of the book asks a lot of questions, to help you to confront the problems that you have identified, to develop your thinking, and to relate your experiences to those of other organisations campaigning against the abuse of small arms – experiences on which this part of the text is based.

Figure 3.1: How Part 3 fits with the rest of the handbook

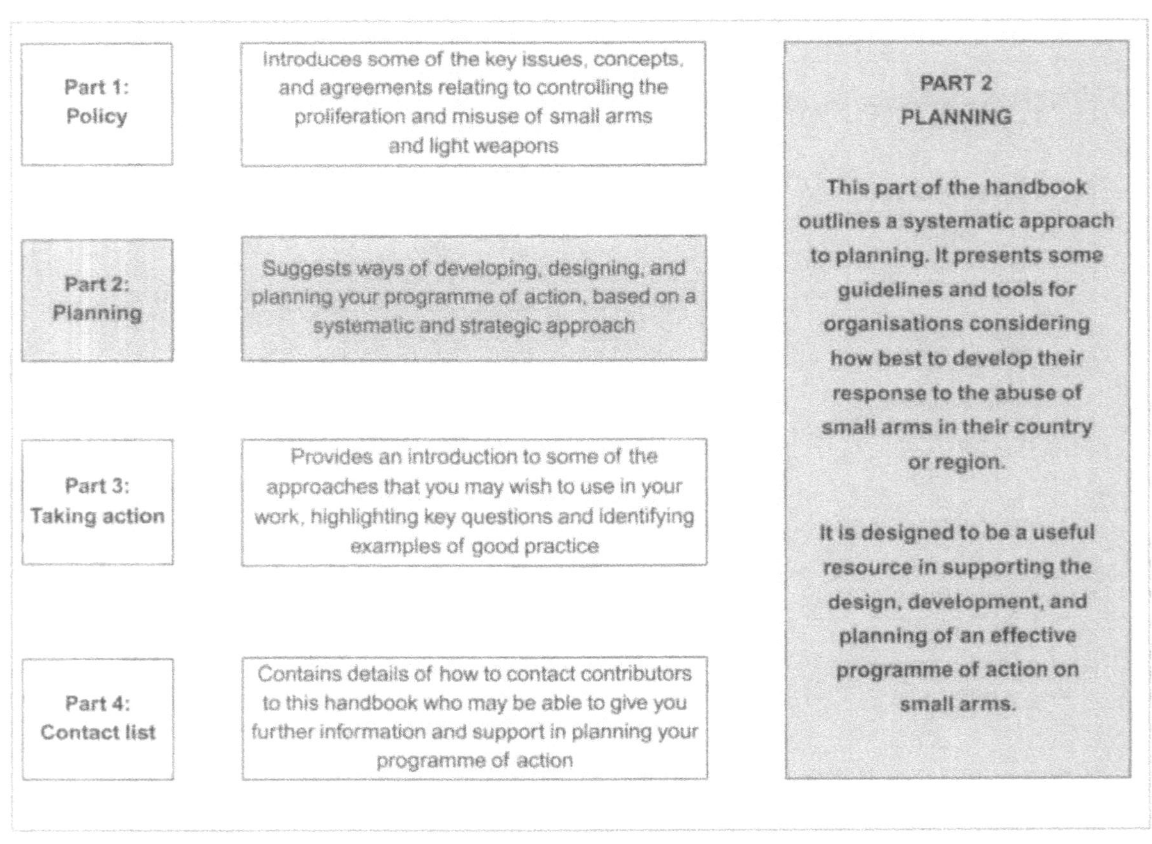

1 Working with others

The problems associated with small arms are international in nature. They might manifest themselves in a particular way in your community, but your problems are linked to those faced by others: in your country, in your region, and around the world.

For example, if your community is affected by insecurity and gun-related violence, that fact is likely to be connected to a lack of national regulation, action, and capacity. This could be made worse by weak border controls in neighbouring countries, allowing small arms to spread into your village. The weapons are often likely to be manufactured in a country many hundreds of miles away, and transported via other countries, using airplanes or ships which are registered elsewhere and operated by companies based in yet another country.

Working together

The international nature of the problem requires that your work should be linked to that of others working on similar issues in other places and at other levels. Where action has been successful on the abuse of small arms in the past, organisations participating in campaigns for change have usually worked in partnership or coalition with others to achieve it.

In addition to presenting a framework to help you to decide *when* to work with others, this section considers *how* you can work with others for change. It is easier to build a momentum for change if organisations work together, rather than in isolation. Of course, this approach carries its own risks, and it is good to be aware of them in order to minimise any potential disadvantages.

Key questions to address

What value can our own organisation add to the actions of others?

- Can we reach a different audience from others?
- Do we have information or access to information that others don't have?
- Do we represent people who would otherwise not have a voice?
- Can we contribute additional skills, expertise, or resources?

Why work together? What are the benefits?

Obviously all situations are different, but joint action offers many benefits:

- Efforts at one level can build on those at another level. For example, analysis presented to high-level institutions is more powerful if informed by local research, personal stories, and individual testimony.
- A range of organisations can speak with a common voice. Their individual credibility and influence are strengthened.
- It is possible to reach a wider range of audiences and policy makers.
- Joint representation may protect those who cannot act alone.
- Civil society is strengthened when knowledge and understanding increase and new relationships and new leadership are forged.
- Funds and other resources can be shared.
- Working together with like-minded institutions and individuals brings strength through unity, moral support, and solidarity.
- Collaboration helps to avoid competition and duplication. Each group can make its own contribution, depending on its particular strengths.

What are the disadvantages, and how can they be minimised?

These are some of the common disadvantages involved in programmes of joint action:

- Co-ordinating collaboration may be time-consuming and distracting.
- It may be difficult to agree clear goals.
- Working together may require groups and organisations to make difficult compromises.
- Conflicts of interests may arise, both internally and externally.
- Individuals or participating groups may not always get credit for their own work.
- The members' distinctive identities may be lost.
- Organisations may have conflicting agendas which are hard to reconcile.
- Participation can be a frustrating, cumbersome, and expensive process.
- If the network breaks down, the credibility of individual members may be damaged.
- Opponents will exploit any opportunity arising from divergence of views.
- Some organisations may tend to dominate the group.

Once you have identified the potential or actual disadvantages, you should think of ways of working that will help to reduce them.

Which organisations should be involved?

Be careful which organisations you choose to work with. Association with trusted, committed organisations can bring credibility to your work and enhance your chances of success. Working with those who have different policies and approaches may be problematic: there is a danger that you could weaken your message in order to find a policy on which you all agree. You should choose allies who complement your overall strategy: are you seeking to build a positive relationship with decision makers, or do you need to challenge them directly through public pressure? Which potential allies fit best with your chosen approach?

What is the best way of working together?

- What are the common goals on which all agree and on which all will work together? (And what are the goals on which individual organisations will continue to work separately?)
- How can the expertise that each organisation offers be put to the best use?
- Is it possible to involve other organisations, for whom the problem of small arms may be a secondary focus?

How will communications and organisation be managed?

Working together, no matter how informally, demands a degree of co-ordination in terms of communication and project organisation. Here are some questions to address:

- What role will our organisation take on?
- Will a loose network be sufficient to achieve our common goals, or will we need a more formal structure, devolving responsibility to an inter-organisation management group to take key decisions?
- How can we make sure that organisations with differing levels of commitment, resources, and capacity can participate on an equal basis?
- Is everyone clear about their roles and responsibilities?
- What communication channels will we use to ensure that people can be kept informed and engaged, even if they don't attend meetings?
- How will we reach decisions? For example, if we need to respond to opportunities quickly, is it acceptable to do this without getting everyone's prior permission?
- How will meetings/information-sharing processes be managed?
- What mechanisms are in place to resolve any conflicts that may emerge?
- Who will take responsibility for keeping things moving?

Case study: building networks in Kibera, Kenya

Kibera in Nairobi is one of the biggest slums in East and Central Africa, housing around one million people. Surrounded by affluent areas of the city, the people of Kibera are generally treated as if they don't exist. Most of their houses are made of mud. There is no police post, no government schools, no power supplies, poor water and sewerage facilities, and virtually no functioning infrastructure. These problems are compounded by constant population pressure, as more people arrive in Nairobi from the villages and find that they cannot get work or earn a living wage. So they end up living in Kibera.

In Kenya, youth groups align themselves to political parties and often, under the guise of offering security, terrorise local people. People do not trust the police to protect them: there is a fear, sometimes realised, that guns recovered by police will find their way back to the criminals. One result of these conditions is that crime is endemic in Kibera and other slums in Kenya, as people fight for scarce resources. Since the mid-1990s there have been clashes between ethnic groups in Kibera. These clashes have had a religious dimension; one tribe was Muslim, one Christian. The government has used coercive measures to try to calm the situation, but without significant efforts at reconciliation.

The Kibera Youth Group emerged in 1999 as a response to these problems and set itself the task of looking for solutions. The group's message to young people – both young Christians and young Muslims – was: 'We are fighting for something which is not our cause'. Youths were fighting on behalf of political leaders, but not gaining anything from it. Young people are seen as the perpetrators of the violence, but they are also its major victims.

In a climate of continuing sporadic violence, Kibera Youth Programme for Peace and Development (KYPPEDE) works to create awareness of local problems and their causes and solutions. Its approach is based on the fundamental principle that young people are best placed to influence other young people. KYPPEDE has undertaken a wide-ranging programme of action. Its multi-faceted approach includes the following initiatives:

- Seeking to encourage dialogue between the police and community groups.
- Promoting community policing and better procedures for managing stockpiles of weapons.
- Establishing networks to give early warning of impending trouble.

- Providing training in conflict management.
- Giving support to the victims of violence.
- Mobilising peace organisations.
- Advocating reforms to the President, the police, and religious leaders.
- Developing skills and creating alternatives to violence.

KYPPEDE recognised that the problem was bigger than any one organisation; so they asked themselves: who can we work with? They engage in networking, from the local to the global levels, in the following ways:

- Participating in local forums involving the local community administration, police officials, and the private sector.
- Combining with community-based organisations in order to gather evidence and conduct research.
- Helping to establish the Nairobi Network for Peace, whose first meeting was attended by youth representatives from more than 100 organisations, from eight constituencies across Nairobi.
- Working with peace groups to help them to incorporate action on small arms in their work.
- Working actively with the National Peace Organisations, seeking to create a country-wide youth movement.
- Building links outside Kenya: for example, through visits to camps, barracks, and rehabilitation centres in Uganda to meet child soldiers and other young people affected by violence.
- Working with IANSA to promote global solutions to the problems of small arms.
- Organising a day of international solidarity at the time of the 2001 UN Conference on Small Arms, involving UN representatives, the Police Commissioner, the Mayor, and others.

The organisation's focus is always on promoting dialogue, based on the conviction that peace cannot be achieved without it.

(This case study was developed with the help of the Kibera Youth Programme for Peace and Development and is based on the members' own experiences and opinions.)

Case study: building an advocacy alliance in the UK

An informal grouping of NGOs working on arms issues in the UK has been in place for a number of years, originally operating as an information-sharing network. More recently, the UK Working Group has evolved from a network into a more coherent advocacy alliance. The UKWG consists of Amnesty International UK, BASIC, Christian Aid, International Alert, Oxfam GB, and Saferworld. Some members are broad-based mass membership/ campaigning organisations; others are smaller, with a focus on research and policy reform. The UKWG now works on a number of different levels:

- Internationally, UKWG members have played a key role in the development of a global small-arms network (IANSA).
- Regionally, the UKWG, in collaboration with partner NGOs in other EU member states, monitors the impact of the EU Code of Conduct on arms exports and encourages EU member states to implement and strengthen the Code.
- Nationally, the UKWG is working to strengthen arms-trade legislation, monitor UK arms exports, and promote transparency and parliamentary accountability.

As a formalised alliance, the UKWG differs from an information network in the following ways:

1. The UKWG has a joint mission statement and a set of jointly agreed aims. These clearly position the members as advocating that the regulation of arms transfers and any lawful uses of arms must be based upon observance of universal human-rights standards and international humanitarian law. This policy means that organisations who campaign for an end to all arms transfers, for example, cannot join the UKWG, although it does not prevent the UKWG from working with those organisations informally.
2. UKWG members seek to act jointly: for example in meetings with government ministers, officials, and parliamentarians and through the issuing of joint briefings and joint press statements. In addition to these combined approaches, individual members contribute according to their particular specialisms, such as local campaigning, or in-depth policy analysis.

The experience of the UKWG members suggests that by working together the organisations involved have achieved more than they could have done individually.

The early stages of the formation of the working group presented many challenges. Each of the component organisations has an individual and distinct profile. The challenge when establishing the group was to identify a strong common focus and to agree that this focus was particular to the work undertaken by members as part of the group, but that membership did not preclude organisations from following their own agendas and from forming other alliances in other areas.

The grouping started as a network and gradually became the UK Working Group. This change in the nature of the way in which the individual organisations worked together occurred to meet the challenges of the external political environment. All the organisations wanted to see a change in UK legislation on arms, and they recognised that the potential for making an impact on the UK government was greater if they worked together than if they worked individually. Each organisation is different, and therefore each has something valuable to contribute to the alliance. The members are able to benefit from each other's strengths, and by acting collectively they can minimise their weaknesses.

Thus the relationship is mutually reinforcing. For example, the policy analysis undertaken by Saferworld can be combined with the legitimacy of an organisation like Oxfam, and the strong membership base of organisations like Amnesty International can enhance the power of collective advocacy.

The UK Working Group has been instrumental in the development and passage of the Arms Export Control Act, which is the first such legislation in the UK since 1938. It is recognised by all organisations that they have benefited from working together, and it is this shared understanding of the value of co-operation which maintains the alliance.

(This case study was developed with the help of the UK Working Group and is based on its experiences and opinions.)

2 Security and risk

As part of your planning process, you have probably analysed the general social, political, and economic environment in which you are working. (See Part 2 of the Handbook.) However, you also need to think about the specific environment in which you will be operating, from the particular perspective of managing security and risk.

It is very important to assess the security situation in which you are working, in terms of both political engagement and the maintenance of personal safety. The questions in this section should help you to make this assessment. However, in the end, only you can decide how much risk your work entails, and the degree of risk that you are willing to accept.

Minimising risks

Risk can be minimised by understanding in detail the environment in which you plan to act. Make sure that you conduct a joint assessment with everyone who is involved in a specific project.

Key questions to address

What risks might be faced?

Risks may arise, for example, from the following sources:

- government, if the availability of arms is being treated as a security issue;
- rebel groups, if, for example, you are perceived as being a 'double agent';
- arms brokers and others with vested interests in maintaining the *status quo*; these groups may have links with organised crime.

Security risks can affect both you as an individual and also your organisation. Risks might include the following:

- theft/robbery/banditry
- traffic 'accidents'
- detention
- hostage-taking/kidnapping
- surveillance/attempts to seize information
- armed attack (e.g. risk of injury from shelling or bombing)
- fabricated scandals to discredit your organisation
- staff targeted for abuse.

To help you to determine the risks, you may need to contact knowledgeable sources, such as:

- researchers
- aid/development NGOs active in the relevant areas
- UN country offices (UNHCR, UNDP)
- embassies and consulates
- media contacts.

Obviously, the levels of risk and the types of security threat vary according to external factors such as geography and timing. And the higher your own profile and the more effective you are, the greater the risk is likely to be. The best advice we can give is that you can never assume that there is no risk.

What measures can be taken to reduce the risks?

It is essential to gather specific, up-to-date information about the potential security risks that may arise as a result of particular interventions you are considering. In addition, you could consider adopting some or all of the following measures:

- establishing and maintaining clear lines of communication
- issuing protective equipment, e.g. bullet-proof clothing
- avoiding travelling alone
- developing specific evacuation plans
- travelling with partners who have relevant skills and experience
- developing good relations with key powerful people who will use their influence if you are threatened
- planning in advance for various possible security threats.

How can your organisation support others, and how can others support you?

Many NGOs working for change on small-arms issues provide an extremely important support service to colleagues. This support function is crucial to maintaining safety and minimising risk in difficult circumstances. Sometimes, developing networks and coalitions can help to formalise a support network through linked strategies and plans. Solidarity techniques include the following:

- campaigns against those who perpetrate the threat
- campaigns though the Internet and letter writing
- demonstrations at embassies and elsewhere
- campaigns in alliance with government and inter-government organisations
- setting up a solidarity fund for victims
- awards/recognitions and other incentives for those working to combat the abuse of small arms.

Case study: peace communities in Colombia

In 1998, Oxfam developed a solidarity campaign to support peace communities in San Jose in Colombia. Members of these communities took positive action to ban the carrying of guns and all assistance to the various armed factions operating in Colombia at the time. The political context in Colombia was so precarious that intimidation, violence, and fear prevented those affected from speaking out. In the first three months of the project, some 37 members of the communities were killed in armed violence. In response, the peace communities sought international support for their initiative.

Oxfam supporters and members of the UK public sent thousands of messages of support to those in danger of being harassed or killed. These messages of solidarity were used to focus international media attention on the forgotten victims of violence. In addition, UK campaign supporters sent letters encouraging the UK government to use its presidency of the European Union to express its support for the peace communities and appeal to armed factions to respect them.

Such solidarity action played a key role in reducing risks of further armed violence in the communities themselves, by reminding the various armed groups to respect the peace communities, knowing that the eyes of the international community were scrutinising their actions.

Two members of the communities have commented: 'We will always be grateful to you [Oxfam]. In San Jose, when we feel alone, we think of all the people who support our community of peace.' ... 'We feel more secure with the international community putting pressure on the gunmen to respect the peace communities.'

Practical guidelines for assessing risk

Risk-assessment checklist

Points to consider in a risk assessment include the following:[1]

Has the risk to personal health and safety of those travelling been assessed?

- Have travellers received the necessary advice on medical precautions, for example on immunisation against infectious disease?
- Have details of any specific security advice or information been gathered?
- Has the previous relevant experience of others been identified?
- Is safety equipment available (protective vests, etc.), and has safety training been provided?
- Are appropriate contingency plans in place?

Have risks relating to the schedule and mode of travel been assessed?

- Have the modes of transport been considered, and the specific risks associated with them, including the normal risks of travel by road or air in the country?
- Have alternative methods of travel been identified?
- Is there a detailed schedule of the trip, with contact telephone numbers identified for each destination? Is there a commitment not to deviate from this schedule?

Is an appropriate evacuation plan in place, and can this plan be implemented promptly and effectively?

- What transport will be used in an emergency? Which routes will be followed? What additional visa requirements might apply if activists were evacuated to a neighbouring country?
- If the plan is dependent on the United Nations, has agreement for evacuation in the event of an emergency been obtained in writing? If not, can contact be made and assurances received as a priority from UN officials on arrival in the country?
- Have all relevant sources of advice at the destination been checked?

Is there an adequate level of control over physical security?

- In general: in the country, city, or region?
- In particular: at venues for meetings, and at accommodation facilities?

Have appropriate communication methods, back-ups, and contacts for travellers been identified?

- Has an individual with leading responsibility for security been identified?
- Is there a list of details of contact people, and has a schedule of regular contacts at agreed dates and times been arranged?
- Is communication equipment available – e.g. satellite phone, mobile phone?
- Do all travellers have a copy of the necessary information about security and addresses of contacts?

3 Gathering information through research

One of the most common problems faced by all governments, NGOs, and community groups is a lack of credible and accurate information about the nature and extent of the small-arms problem in their area. Research will help you to understand these problems and to assess which approaches have or have not worked in response to the problem of small arms in various situations.

Reliable information on small arms is often hard to find. Data may be treated as secret by governments and other institutions. Even in the European Union, for example, where the EU Code of Conduct on arms places a political obligation on all member states to publish an annual report on arms sales, the Dutch government is currently the only one that makes available detailed information on licence applications that it has refused.

However, conducting research on small arms is not always so difficult: officially published and secondary sources of information are often available – if you look in the right place. One visit to a newsagent's shop in Warsaw, Poland, for example, led to the discovery of more than ten magazine advertisements for electric-shock weapons.

Some people think of research as an academic activity; but for planning purposes, research need not be of academic quality. Often all that is needed is a careful analysis of the environment in which the planned activities will be taking place. In other situations, the quality of your research may help to determine your legitimacy and authority to speak on a particular issue. It can help you to demonstrate the reasons why change is needed

There are basically three different types of research. They each have a different purpose, and may differ also in the kind of evidence that is collected, and the way in which the findings are presented. See Figure 3.2. These approaches are not mutually exclusive. For example, sometimes an effort to understand the problem better may provide the basis for policy recommendations that influence others to change.

Figure 3.2: Three different types of research

Understanding the problem or context	Monitoring and evaluation	Advocacy research
Collecting and analysing information in order to identify and understand a problem or the wider context	Assessing your progress towards meeting your objectives, or how the work of others has affected the situation	Research whose findings and conclusions are presented in ways that seek to influence others to change
See, for example, the range of findings that led the Working Group on Weapons Reduction in Cambodia to identify the key problems facing the country and the region (p.78 of this book)	*See, for example, the range of measures established by Viva Rio to assess the success of their project to reduce firearms violence in the State of Rio de Janeiro (p.132 of this book)*	*See, for example, the sections relating to lobbying and audiences and communication for more details on the importance and use of advocacy research.*

Research: key questions to address

If you don't have enough information about the problems facing you and the people on whose behalf you are working, you may need to conduct additional research. Sometimes you may need to commission others to do the research on your behalf. The following questions should help you when shaping, conducting, and presenting your research:

What do we want the research for?

Think clearly at the outset about what you hope to achieve or find out by doing a particular piece of research. Make sure that the research is directly relevant to your organisation and its goals. For example:

- What, in precise terms, is the problem that we want the research to address?
- What are the goals and objectives of the research?
- What do we want to find out? Why? (Prepare a list of questions or a framework for the research.)
- What constraints might we face in doing the research? Are there concerns about security and risks?
- Is new research really needed? (Maybe someone else has already done it!)
- What are our likely audiences: what kinds of information and quality of evidence will they each need?

Always be prepared to challenge your initial assumptions or hypothesis when you develop your research plan.

How will evidence be gathered?

Ensure that your research is designed with a particular purpose in mind. Ensure too that your research is credible, reasoned, and well argued. For example:

- How will the information be gathered? What sort of data? From what sources? (Where possible, you should seek to use original information, collected directly from those affected by the issue, or from officially published material which you can cite.)
- Who should be approached? Which people? Which groups?
- How will bias be avoided? Will issues be analysed from the perspective of groups who may be affected in different ways? For example: men and women, children and older people, disabled people, members of different ethnic or religious groups.
- What techniques will be used?
- What is the budget?
- What is the timetable?

Who should do the research?

- Should it be done by our own organisation, or do we need to work with other experts and researchers?
- If it is proposed to commission a research team, can we ensure that members contribute different kinds of experience: will there be an even balance between men and women, and a balance of backgrounds?
- If others are commissioned to do the research, who will be accountable for each aspect of it?
- Are there security-related reasons for using specialist researchers?

How will data be collected?

- Will the data be reliable and valid? Can the information be cross-checked from different sources?
- Have we made provision for the security of researchers collecting data in violence-prone communities?
- Have we recorded (and cited, where appropriate) the sources of the data used?
- Are we sure that our research techniques are free from bias? (For example, when using questionnaires, researchers should not ask leading questions, which encourage people to answer in a certain way. They should be aware that interviewees may give biased or deliberately inaccurate information; so all data should be validated by questioning people with a variety of backgrounds and perspectives.)
- Are all members of a community able to participate in the research process? Times and techniques might disadvantage certain groups. Should men and women be interviewed separately, for example, to prevent men from dominating discussions?

- Can we obtain documentary evidence of events: video footage, photographs, and taped interviews, for example, to supplement written testimony?

How will the data be analysed and evaluated?

- Do we want the researchers simply to present the facts, or do we want them to interpret them too?
- Does the analysis relate back to the objectives that we set in the research brief?
- Is it clear how the data have led to particular conclusions?
- Does the analysis demonstrate how the conclusions have been verified? For example, it should show that information, particularly qualitative information, has been cross-checked.

How will the research report be presented?

- The content and style of the report must be appropriate for the intended audiences.
- Data should be presented in accessible formats (tables, graphs, etc.).
- The report should include a summary of the main findings, conclusions, and recommendations.
- It should contain an explanation of the research methodology (short and simple, unless the research is for an academic audience).
- Exposing or accusing private individuals or companies may lead to legal action for libel and defamation. It is essential to have absolute proof of guilt when making specific allegations against named targets.
- People who have supplied information should not be put at risk.
- How will the results of the research be shared more widely? Publishing a report is rarely enough to influence decision makers. It is important to develop a dissemination strategy, to include private lobbying meetings based on the report, and perhaps a media launch.

Primary and secondary data, and possible sources

Two types of data are used in research:

- information especially collected for the research project: so-called 'primary data'
- information which has already been published: so-called 'secondary data'.

Table 3.1: Sources of data for research on small arms and light weapons

Types of primary data	**Some sources of primary data**
Informal comments and reactions	• Listening to what different people are saying in different situations • Watching how people behave in different situations
Semi-structured qualitative input	• Recording oral histories • Conducting surveys and presenting questionnaires • Conducting interviews, discussions, and workshops with individuals and groups • Using ranking and scoring exercises to identify people's priorities • Using pictures and maps to stimulate community discussions
Quantified data	• Questionnaires and surveys
Results of action learning	• Piloting small-scale solutions, with rigorous monitoring of results, to persuade decision makers to implement similar solutions more widely
Types of secondary data	**Some sources of secondary data**
Official import and export data	• Government reports on arms sales, e.g.UK government figures (www.fco.gov.uk) • The Federation of American Scientists provides excellent information on US arms sales (www.fas.org/asmp/library/handbook/cover.html)
Hospital records	• Try the World Health Organisation website (www.who.int/violence_injury_prevention/) • Or the International Physicians for the Prevention of Nuclear War (www.ippnw.org/)
UN reports	• See the website of the UN Department for Disarmament Affairs (http://disarmament.un.org/)
NGO research reports	Many NGOs produce reports on small arms, including: • Small Arms Survey (www.smallarmssurvey.org/) • Saferworld (www.saferworld.org.uk) • International Alert (www.international-alert.org/) • Oxfam GB (www.oxfam.org.uk) • Amnesty International (www.amnesty.org) • Human Rights Watch (www.hrw.org/arms/) • Bonn International Centre for Conversion (BICC) (www.bicc.de/) • NISAT (www.nisat.org) • Federation of American Scientists (www.fas.org) • For more information, visit the IANSA website (www.iansa.org)
Arms-trade monitoring agencies	• SIPRI (www.sipri.se) • US Congressional Research Service Report (www.fas.org/asmp/resources/govern/crs-rl31529.pdf) • Small Arms Survey (www.smallarmssurvey.org/)
Government or international commissions of inquiry	• Try the UN Department of Disarmament Affairs for UN reports (http://disarmament.un.org/)
Press reports	• Many media outlets (national, regional, or international) have websites carrying small-arms features. IANSA's news section and news archive are good starting points (www.iansa.org/news/index.htm)
Specialist media and special interest journals	• Jane's Defence Weekly (www.janes.com/) • Defence News (www.defencenews.com/)
Academic research and specialist researchers	• Organisations such as Saferworld, International Alert, Small Arms Survey, Amnesty International, and Oxfam can provide contacts with small-arms specialists
Parliamentary scrutiny	• Some parliaments or committees of parliamentarians analyse small-arms issues. Some hold hearings in public and produce reports

Company records and databases	Company records are often accessible. They can be found in the following places in the following countries; you can find links to the same information for other countries at www.companieshouse.gov.uk/ • Australia: Australian Securities and Investments Commission (www.asic.gov.au/asic/asic.nsf) • Brazil: Departamento Nacional de Registro do Comércio (www.facil.dnrc.gov.br/) • Cambodia: Ministry of Commerce (www.moc.gov.kh/) • Czech Republic: Czech Ministry of Finance (wwwinfo.mfcr.cz/) • Latvia: Latvijas Republikas Uznemumu Registras (www.ur.gov.lv/index.php) • Spain: Colegio de Registradores de la Propiedad y Mercantiles de España (www.registradores.org/castellano/comunes/home.html) • South Africa: Companies and Intellectual Property Registration Office (www.cipro.gov.za/) • UK: Companies House (www.companieshouse.gov.uk/) • USA: Corporate Registrations in the United States of America (http://ws1.companies-house.gov.uk/ias/usa_sites_-_english_frameset.html)
Promotional material	• Brochures and promotional material produced by manufacturers and dealers. Information produced by the organisers of arms fairs.
Firearms-ownership data	• Police and other licensing authorities
Personal testimony of those involved or affected	For an example of personal testimonies, try: • Amnesty International (www.amnesty.org) • Oxfam GB (www.oxfam.org.uk/policy/papers/drc/congo.pdf)

See Part 4 of this handbook for a more comprehensive list of useful organisations.

No single research method is without bias. To make the research as objective as possible, you should use a set of different research techniques, both qualitative and quantitative, and then cross-check your findings.

4 Obtaining funds

Your ability to deliver your programme of action will depend on your ability to obtain funding. Competition for funds is great, so you will have a key advantage if you understand how funding processes work and what donors are looking for. Donors are more likely to fund your project if you can demonstrate that you are working with others – or at least that you will not duplicate the work of others.

This section introduces a range of practical suggestions to help you to identify funders, write a fundraising proposal, and write reports to donors. However, in addition to support in the form of grants from donors, there are many other possible funding options, which include the following.

- **Membership funding:** Some organisations invite individuals to become members, in return for a membership fee. Organisations such as Amnesty International, with a large supporter base, can raise a significant proportion of their income in this way.
- **Regular donations by individuals:** Some organisations, such as Saferworld, have supporters who regularly donate money, often on a monthly basis. They also depend on legacies, and one-off donations by post or by credit card via the Internet or telephone.
- **Street collections:** The Red Cross, like many organisations, raises a significant portion of its funding by collecting money from people on the street. This approach has been successfully adapted by some organisations who collect donations from local businesses to fund their work: the Forum for Civic Initiative (FIQ-FCI), for example, an NGO based in Kosovo.
- **Merchandising:** It is also possible to raise money through the sale of merchandise, although this usually requires a level of expertise in commerce or business. Oxfam is one example of an organisation that raises money in this way, through its shops, catalogues, and on-line sales.
- **Events:** Adopt A Minefield raises money by organising an annual event called The Night of the Thousand Dinners, when people pay to enjoy a meal cooked and hosted by someone in their local community. Many organisations raise funds by sponsored events, such as a marathon walk; participants persuade their friends to pay them to take up the challenge.

Practical guidelines for securing funding

1 Do your research. Try to identify all possible funders and their interests.

2 Compile a list of the donors that appear most likely to support your project.

3 Choose prospective funders by examining their descriptive profiles and recent histories of grant-making. Make sure that you research their restrictions before you approach them.

4 Research the donor's existing projects to gain an idea of their likely character.

5 Look for foundations that have already supported projects similar to yours, or those based in your geographic area.

6 When identifying potential sources of funding, think how you could match your priorities to the donors' interests. Think how you could frame your project so that it links to related issues such as development and peace-building, which may be the prime concerns of the potential funders.

7 Send appropriately customised requests to a few prospective donor organisations.

8 Take account of the application deadline of each funder, and make your plans accordingly.

9 Try to submit your proposal six to nine months before your programme is to be implemented. This will allow you time to apply elsewhere if you are not successful.

10 Be realistic in your expectations. Do not make the mistake of focusing all your efforts on one 'ideal' funder. Even the most experienced proposal writers will receive many letters of rejection before securing a grant.

Table 3.2: Some potential sources of funds for action against the abuse of small arms

Governments	
United Kingdom Department for International Development	www.dfid.gov.uk
Swedish Ministry for Foreign Affairs	www.ud.se
Netherlands Ministry of Foreign Affairs	www.minbuza.nl/english/homepage.asp
Canadian Ministry of Foreign Affairs	www.dfait-maeci.gc.ca
UN agencies	
United Nations Development Programme (UNDP)	www.undp.org
United Nations Department of Disarmament Affairs (UNDDA)	www.un.org/Depts/dda/
International NGOs	
IANSA	www.iansa.org
Oxfam GB	www.oxfam.org.uk
World Council of Churches	www.wcc-coe.org/
Foundations and trusts	
The Ford Foundation	www.fordfound.org
The Rockefeller Foundation	www.rockfound.org
Ploughshares Fund	www.ploughshares.org
Soros Foundations Network	www.soros.org
Earned income	
Membership fees, merchandising, shops, events	

(See Part 4 of this handbook for a more comprehensive list of useful organisations.)

Sources of funding – and their implications

Consider the political implications of potential sources of funding.

- What does the donor hope to gain from the relationship?
- Will the donor introduce conditions that limit your freedom of action?
- Does the donor have sufficient sensitivity and local knowledge to be able to understand the context in which your organisation is operating?
- Is the donor likely to interfere in your organisation's work, or to influence the type of programme that you operate, or the way in which you deliver and measure it? If so, what negative consequences might be implied?
- Could a prospective donor be a useful channel of political influence, as well as a source of funding?

Writing a proposal for funding

An increasing number of funders prefer to receive a brief letter of inquiry concerning the suitability of a project *before* a full proposal is submitted. This initial contact should briefly indicate all the elements that would eventually be part of a proposal (programme goals, objectives, and activities, timetable, estimated costs, methods of monitoring and evaluation, etc.).

The relevance of the proposal to the agenda of the prospective funder should be made very clear. Your proposal must show how your project fits a funder's pattern of giving. If a donor provides guidelines on the format of a proposal, you should follow them closely. Table 3.3 summarises the elements of a good funding proposal.

Table 3.3: What to include in a funding proposal

		Links to other parts of the handbook
Summary	• a brief statement of the overall aim of your programme; • a short description of the project in question; • an explanation of the amount of money required for the project; and • a brief description of your organisation.	
Rationale	This section should provide an explanation of the need for your project. • Define the specific problems that you want to address, and support your argument with evidence and statistics. • Try to demonstrate that your project is workable: that it can be done within a reasonable time, by you, and with a reasonable amount of money. • Avoid exaggeration and excessively emotional appeals. • Refer to the work of others in this field and explain how your work complements, but does not duplicate, their work.	Framing the issue (pp. 98–100)
Objectives	• What are the anticipated outcomes of the project? • Your objectives must be specific, measurable, and achievable in a specified time period. Don't promise what you can't deliver.	Setting objectives (pp. 117–121)
Project partners	• Who are the project partners? • What is the division of responsibility between them and you?	Working with others (pp. 141–7)
Methods and activities	• What will the project actually do? • How it will be conducted?	Influence maps (pp. 113–15)
Project timetable	• What are the major activities, and when will they take place? • Estimate the time-scale in months if you cannot give precise dates. • Include the points when evaluation and report writing will take place.	Creating a Gantt timeline (pp. 124–6)
Staffing needs	• Which staff will be deployed on the project, and for how much of their time?	
Budgeting	• Bear in mind the restrictions of the funder (e.g. some refuse to fund salaries) and compensate in your budget accordingly. • For most projects, costs should be grouped into sub-categories (see the section on finance and budgeting). • If costs are simple and obvious, narrative explanations are unnecessary.	Developing an action plan (pp. 122–3)

Monitoring and evaluation	• Who will monitor the activities during the project time-frame? • How will activities be monitored? • What criteria will you use to measure the difference that has been made?	Monitoring and evaluation (pp. 128–38)
Description of your organisation	Briefly outline: • when your organisation came into existence; • its mission, and how your proposal relates to that mission; • the organisation's structure, programmes, and special expertise; • staffing, including the numbers of full-time and part-time staff, and their levels of expertise.	
Conclusion	Summarise your case and try to end with a powerful appeal for your project.	

Writing reports to funders

In order to produce progress reports and project-evaluation reports, it is essential to establish and maintain rigorous monitoring systems. (See the section on monitoring in Part 2.) If a donor provides guidelines on what the format of a report should look like, follow them closely.

Table 3.4: What to include in a funding report

Progress report	• Outline the progress (or lack of progress) of your project so far. Funders want to be sure that you have completed the activities that you included in your funding proposal. • Demonstrate how you have used the criteria for monitoring and evaluation that you described in your proposal.
Variances and proposed changes to the action plan	• Give explicit information about variances from the proposal – activities not completed, or progress not achieved – and give the reasons. • Explain explicitly what you will do differently in order to reach your objectives.
Lessons learned	• Identify any lessons learned from the successes and failures of your project so far.
The future	• Building on the conclusions of your previous sections, explain how you intend to maximise the effectiveness of your activities in the future.

5 Audiences and communications

Persuading decision makers to initiate reforms usually involves a number of techniques. In different political situations and at different times, different approaches will be more appropriate; but some principles always apply.

Defining audiences and the appropriate means of communicating with them

Whenever you act, you are *communicating with an audience*. This is true whether you are targeting a government minister, a journalist, a local community group, or a potential donor. In all cases, you need to deliver your messages in relevant and effective ways. To do this, you will need to set clear goals, identifying which audiences you are communicating with, and why. For each specific audience, both the message and the ways of delivering it will be different. The identification of potential audiences should be part of your planning process. You will choose specific audiences at different times as a way of delivering the message that you wish to communicate to your target or decision maker. These audiences are your *channels of influence* to help you to achieve your objectives.

For more advice on identifying audiences and decision makers, see also the sections in Part 2 on identifying stakeholders and devising an influencing strategy.

Key questions to address

Research your audiences: don't base your communications on assumptions. Ask yourself the following questions.

WHO are the various audiences that we want to reach?

Different groups have very different impacts on the state of affairs that you are seeking to change. And all kinds of factors – such as geography, demographics (age, gender, education, etc.), attitudes, and lifestyle – affect people's response to your messages. 'The public' is not a single group with consistent characteristics and opinions; it includes, for example, women, men, children, politically active people, civil servants, businessmen, and trade unionists. As precisely as possible, you should define the specific audiences whom you will target.

WHY are we communicating with them?

- What change in this audience do we want to bring about?
- Do we need them to *know, believe, say,* or *do* something differently?
- How will this help us to achieve our goals and objectives?

WHAT do they know and care about?

WHAT are the messages that will work best with this specific audience?

WHAT do we want to say to them?

- What do they already know about the issue or situation of concern to us?
- How sympathetic are they likely to be to our concerns?
- What things do they care about? (Not simply in relation to small arms.)
- How can we describe the issue in their language and on their terms?
- What kinds of message might mean something to those audiences?
- Have we told them what we want them to do, why it is important, and why action is needed *now*?
- Can we test our messages with sample groups from the target audience before using them more widely?

HOW will we reach them?

- Do they listen to radio, read newspapers, or watch television?
- Where else do they obtain their information? Whom do they listen to and respect? What has changed their opinions in the past?
- What groups do they belong to?

Practical guidelines for communicating with various audiences

As noted above, in developing your communications programme, you should consider how different audiences may listen to and be interested in different types of message. A simple way to think about various audiences is to consider three distinct groups:

- policy makers and opinion formers
- other groups and individuals who are interested in the issue
- the wider public.

Different messages will be appropriate for these different audiences. At one end of the spectrum, when engaging with policy makers and opinion formers, you should probably target small numbers of people, using very detailed arguments. But you may first need to reach them with simpler messages about your legitimacy to speak out on the issue, building your relationship with them to the point at which you can meet and discuss the arguments in detail. (See also the section on lobbying in this part of the handbook.)

At the other end of the spectrum, in trying to promote your messages to general audiences who may not initially have a reason to be interested, you will need to attract the attention of large numbers of people. This could require a variety of popular approaches, using stories, pictures, or simple and easily accessible slogans and 'sound-bites' through the media. It might help you to obtain the endorsement of famous people or community leaders; or to work directly through communities with music and drama. Or you may choose to train activists who themselves train others to spread the messages, or work through a key group such as a teachers' union, whose members themselves communicate with a wide audience in their daily work.

A communications strategy might therefore look something like the one shown in Figure 3.3.

Figure 3.3: Devising a communications strategy to end the abuse of small arms

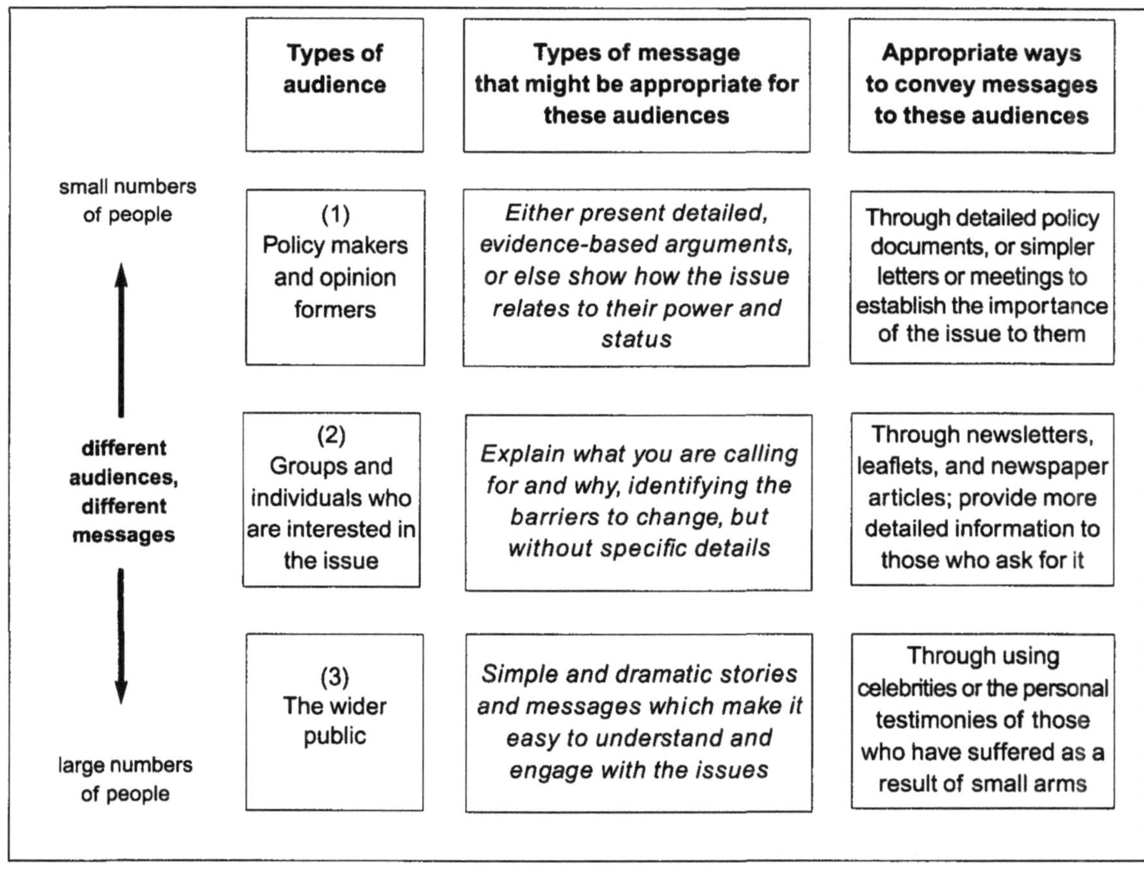

Case study: public-awareness campaign developed by the Serbia and Montenegro Red Cross

Drastic political changes in the territory of the former Yugoslavia, involving many armed conflicts and the dissolution of the former State, altered the social fabric of the country. Economic, political, and social instability led to growing levels of insecurity. People felt the need to increase their own personal security, and the easy availability of small arms offered them an obvious tool. A deterioration in the rule of law accelerated the process. Levels of criminality rose, numbers of gun victims increased, traditional moral values disappeared, and attitudes towards weapons, especially among young people, shifted radically. It became very popular to own and even use a pistol or some other weapon, and to show it off in public places. More and more people bought weapons to protect themselves, and more and more people were dying or being seriously injured.

In keeping with its mandate, the Serbia and Montenegro Red Cross identified an opportunity to influence public opinion regarding the acceptability of the new 'gun culture'. The primary audience for its campaign, 'For life – without weapons', was established as young people. This was because the youth were both perpetrators and victims of gun crime. The campaign seeks to convince young people that having a weapon is not a feature of a modern civilised society, and that a gun is a source of insecurity, rather than security. The campaign aims to offer young people other ways of expending their energy: by participation in sport, arts, and social life.

In thinking about how to reach and communicate with young people, the campaign identified several even more specific target groups:

- teachers and university professors
- schoolchildren
- students of secondary schools
- students of universities
- youth in general.

Messages, slogans, and ways of reaching these different audiences were then developed. For example:

- Thanks to work with the Ministry of Education, it was agreed that, for five weeks in more than 1,500 schools, five to ten minutes of the first class on Monday mornings were devoted to small-arms problems.
- Messages from famous opinion formers regarded as good examples for young people, including sportsmen and women, actors, and

singers, were communicated through TV and billboard advertising.

- In preparation for the traditional New Year's Eve celebrations, which always involved the firing of guns, 50,000 coasters carrying the campaign slogan were produced for use in coffee bars in Belgrade.

The campaign continues. Results to date include the following:

- The campaign has raised awareness of the problem of small arms, putting the issue on the public agenda.
- Public authorities and various ministries have shown their support for the campaign's aims.
- A pledge by the former Yugoslav delegation at the UN Conference on Small Arms to publicly destroy a quantity of weapons was partly fulfilled, with the destruction of 51,000 pieces of small arms in the presence of media and representatives from foreign countries.
- Anecdotal evidence suggests that the volume of shooting on New Year's Eve was much reduced.

Lessons learned

As a result of its public education work, the Serbia and Montenegro Red Cross has identified the following important conclusions to inform its future programmes:

- **Timing:** the campaign must be very carefully planned, to avoid competing with other activities.
- **People:** the key resource in the public-awareness campaign was highly motivated and well-informed speakers and representatives.
- **Approaches:** it is essential to use a range of diverse communication techniques.
- **Encouragement:** in addition to presenting sound arguments, some kind of attractive offer has to be made to people, especially the young.
- **Messages:** use common, modern, and understandable language, adjusted to suit the various target groups. All messages must be short, clear, and effective.
- **Materials** must be attractive, with modern design.

(This case study is based on the experiences and opinions of the Serbia and Montenegro Red Cross.)

6 Mobilising support

There may be times when it is important that significant numbers of people support you and are prepared to show their support for your goals. In some political situations, this will not be possible (for security reasons); and in some contexts it may not be productive (because governments and decision makers may not be influenced by such tactics). But in other situations and at certain times, mass support can be an effective way of increasing the pressure on a decision maker or ensuring that change comes about at the community level. In such circumstances, achieving your goals may require changes in the attitudes or behaviour of key sections of the population.

The approaches that you use will depend on your goals, your audiences, and the political context. In each situation it is important to think carefully about what type of approach will be most effective. The wrong approach at the wrong time could actually damage the legitimacy of your organisation and the chances of your action being successful. For example, a show of concern by only a small number of people may seem to show that the issue is not a political priority, because very few people care about it.

When you plan to convince a decision maker by demonstrating public support for your issue, think about the following:

- What do we want to achieve?
- How much support from people do we need?
- How much preparation time will we need?

This section presents a range of practical guidelines for mobilising support. However, on this subject, above all, local knowledge about what works best is often most valuable. We offer three case studies which illustrate how organisations have mobilised local communities to take action on the abuse of small arms. All three demonstrate how local knowledge, combined with skill and imagination, can be used to achieve change.

Practical guidelines for mobilising support

Effective public action

Table 3.5: Techniques for effective action

Petitions	• A simple way for people to show support for your cause. • May also be used as a way of generating extra media publicity.
Demonstrations of protest	• May be news-worthy: issue a news release and offer to provide a spokesperson to explain why the demonstration is being held. • At the protest itself, use strong and simple visual images (with minimal text) which will look good on TV and in the newspapers. • Music and noise help to attract attention and motivate people. • Act peacefully: don't advocate approaches which put people at risk. • Be aware of the law and how to act in order to stay within it: breaking the law can undermine your legitimacy.
Public meetings	• Can be used as an opportunity for getting your message across. • Think about how to motivate those attending to take follow-up action in support of your aims. • You may be able to set up a stall or display at public meetings or events organised by related groups.
Public-access radio	• Phone-ins or discussion programmes may provide opportunities for key supporters to discuss your issue in public or challenge others who are opposing your messages.
Internet	• Using the Internet allows you to control what you say and how you say it, and gives you global reach, instantly. • Internet technology works best when it *supplements* traditional communication techniques, not when used as a substitute. • You will need to devise ways for your supporters to take action through the Internet: do you have the email addresses of your key decision makers? Are there discussion forums which you could join? • But there are significant cultural, social, political and economic barriers to Internet usage. Be careful not to widen the 'digital divide' between rich and poor.
Community mobilisation	• Community-level analysis of the issue and its impact could be introduced through workshops and drama. • This may lead to direct action to solve the problems, or to lobbying sessions involving both community leaders and decision makers.

Case study: Conscientious Objectors in Bosnia (COIB)

The problem identified by COIB is that there is no alternative to military service for young Bosnian men who object to taking up and using a gun. The organisation seeks the introduction of a fair system of civilian service which operates without discrimination against those who choose to take part in it.

COIB identified three barriers against resolving this problem:

- The law in Bosnia gives insufficient attention to the notion of civilian service.
- Public awareness of the concept of civilian service is very low.
- It is commonly assumed that 'You're not a man if you don't serve in the army', and that any dilution of the army's strength could threaten national security.

COIB has focused its efforts on removing the first two of these barriers. It has tried, so far without success, to address the third barrier by framing the issue as a question of freedom of choice, rather than one of opposition to the army.

Politically, COIB is working with and through federal and national parliaments and relevant ministries, including Defence, Justice, Social Care, and Education. Its political strategy is designed to access and influence representatives from the various different political currents.

The second strand of action has been to promote public awareness and action. Research before the launch of the campaign revealed very low awareness of the idea of civilian service. The target group for the campaign was established as men between the ages of 15 and 25. COIB chose to reach this audience through intensive, continuous work in the major cities and related, smaller actions in the smaller cities.

Campaigners arrive in a place, recruit support, and then get active – erecting book stalls, holding lectures, displaying posters, distributing leaflets, making as many contacts as possible. The idea is to organise interesting activities which reach the biggest possible audience and gain attention from the media. For example, on one occasion, twenty street actions took place at the same time across the country, as a symbol of youth acting together. On another occasion, on the first day of Spring – a day that is identified as heralding peace – COIB established a presence at crossroads in the big cities. In a two-hour action, promotional materials were distributed, petitions signed, and questionnaires completed. Support was given to those people who expressed an interest in applying for civilian service, rather than military service. As a result, surpassing all expectations, hundreds of people have applied: 150 people visited the organisation's offices, and 500 applied on the streets.

COIB has kept meticulous records of its activities and outputs. This has made it possible to make a strong case that the outcomes noted below have resulted from, or been heavily influenced by, COIB's own actions:

- Applications for civilian service rose from only a handful before the launch of the campaign to more than 250 in the last six months of 2002.
- Research has shown that awareness of the concept of civilian service among the target population has risen tenfold.
- The campaign has been recognised by the international community and by politicians operating at various levels of government.
- There has been a policy change within various State bodies: for example, the Ministry of Justice has established a Civilian Commission.
- Fifty organisations have been approved for participation in the civilian service programme.

Despite these successes, at the time of writing the Ministry of Defence has yet to sign a single contract with those organisations that have expressed willingness to take part in the scheme. The next phase in the campaign is to work for the drafting of a new law on civilian service, in accordance with European standards and human-rights law – and then to ensure that it is enacted.

(This case study is based on the experiences and opinions of Conscientious Objectors in Bosnia.)

Box 18: Working with grassroots communities – notes from a consultation workshop in West Africa

A consultation workshop was hosted by the Foundation for Security and Development in Africa (FOSDA), Mouvement Contre Les Armes Légères in Afrique de l'Oest (MALAO), and the Centre for Democratic Empowerment (CEDE) in Senegal in 2002. There follows a summary of the discussions that took place there.

- Social change is not just about broadening the conditions for participation and improving the functioning of the State. It is also about strengthening civil society itself.

- Community conscientisation is the process of bringing together groups and organisations to raise people's awareness of and demand for particular solutions. This approach involves community members critically reflecting on their experiences, becoming aware of a problem, and identifying it as a high priority for community action. This may lead to action on chosen courses, involving many strategic allies, at all levels, in a wide range of support activities.
- This participative, grassroots approach provides the local community with skills and a sense of ownership of the campaign.

Methodology, challenges, and obstacles

- The vital first step is to conduct participatory research through surveys and discussions with community groups, in order to understand the social relevance of your campaign to the community with which you hope to work. Your solutions must not be (or be perceived to be) externally imposed.
- A priority is to identify and involve key targets, e.g. traditional leaders, State representatives, and community-based organisations (including religious groups, age groups, trade unions, women's groups, armed groups in conflict areas, civil defence groups, NGOs).
- The participative approach uses a lot of resources, so your programme should be planned accordingly.
- Community mobilisation often works best as a complement to policy influencing, rather than as an alternative to it. But in some cases, community-level action can begin to solve problems directly, where governments have failed. [See, for example, the case study below on PPDI.]

Common problems include the following:

- Cultural differences may emerge between the campaigning organisation and the local community.
- Lack of local community knowledge may act as a barrier to progress.
- Lack of clarity about the possible outcomes and how they might benefit the community will also obstruct progress.
- The community may tend to protect its own members, resenting external interference.
- Community members may feel personally insecure about any change.

One way to manage these challenges is to gain the support of influential champions of change within the communities themselves. They will be able to give legitimacy to the activities promoted by outsiders.

Where the community has resorted to guns, we should seek to increase our own understanding – and their understanding – of the often complex, interlinking causal factors, which may include the following:

- economic insecurity
- suspicions between the community and the security forces
- bad governance, making the community feel marginalised
- a collapsing State – and hence the absence of any State security force
- the absence, or perceived absence, of social justice.

Case study: Pastoralist Peace and Development Initiative (PPDI)

When civil war and anarchy broke out in Somalia in the early 1990s, large numbers of refugees and their livestock fled over the border into northern Kenya. Natural resources such as water, pasture, and firewood were insufficient to cope with the new demands. The widespread proliferation of small arms in Somalia was one of the major factors that led people to flee to Kenya. Some of the refugees brought arms with them, and used them to gain control of waterholes and wells, denying water to weaker or unarmed clans and family groups.

The guns gave their owners prestige and created fear. They also brought economic and commercial benefits, because there was money to be made in selling arms to local livestock owners, and even in Nairobi. Local clans who had traditionally used spears in conflicts with their neighbours now armed themselves with guns to protect their property, bartering livestock for small arms. Killings, robberies, and rape became a daily occurrence. Travel became increasingly difficult and dangerous. Women and children lost husbands and fathers. Traditional custom dictated that warring parties should spare women and elders, but now everyone was vulnerable to violence. Clan fights proliferated. Everybody was an actual or potential loser, because even the man making money from selling arms faced the prospect of one day meeting his enemy.

Traditional means of conflict resolution were breaking down. The government had set up new political structures to rival traditional systems in which community elders were responsible for resolving conflict; but these new bodies were not answerable to their communities, and the government's security agents found that they could not provide security for its citizens. Government officials were being murdered for their weapons. These factors created a vicious cycle of violence, insecurity, and chronic underdevelopment.

PPDI was established with the goal of achieving sustainable peace and development in the region through active community participation and involvement. Its aim was to promote conflict resolution and peace building. Because the easy availability of guns was intensifying the conflict, PPDI focused on tackling the proliferation of small arms.

PPDI's approach has been founded on respect for and understanding of traditional ways of life. PPDI arranged meetings with warring clans in the region and facilitated the formation of cross-border district peace committees to oversee peace building and to re-establish control over the movement of arms across their borders. The committees consisted of elders, women, and young people from clans living on both sides of the border, along with government officials.

These measures proved workable, due to the way of life of the communities. The population of the area is mostly Somali, a very distinct ethnic entity, distinguished by language, culture, and lifestyle from much of the rest of the Kenyan population. Clan elders represent their communities and proved to be very important in initiating the recovery of illegal small arms from the warring clans, acting as law-makers in their own clans.

The process has helped to revive traditional methods of conflict resolution by which 'blood money' was raised by opposing clans to compensate for lost lives, instead of revenge being sought. Another key element has been the degree of co-operation with provincial government. Despite an initial lack of trust on the part of the communities, PPDI recognised that government involvement was vital to achieving progress, and it has worked to give support and encouragement to government representatives.

The project's successes have been founded on patience, dialogue, and co-operation. Despite the difficulty of raising funds, PPDI's progress to date has produced the following results:

- a marked reduction in violence in the region;
- improved relationships between government officials and representatives of civil society, especially the community leaders;
- the voluntary surrender of thousands of illegal arms by community members;
- improved cross-border co-operation with communities living across the Somali border, thus minimising the spill-over of small arms and tension from Somalia into Kenya.

(This case study has been developed by the Pastoralist Peace and Development Initiative and is based on their experiences and opinions.)

7 Lobbying

Lobbying is likely to be an important element of your work, whether you are talking to your target directly, or indirectly through the channels (the routes of influence) that you have identified. Lobbying is often perceived as a complex and difficult exercise; but you can easily develop your skills, if you break it down into its two key components: relationship building and negotiation.

Too often, lobbying is seen as a matter of debating eloquently – whereas it is in fact rare for decision makers to change their mind purely as a result of the forcefulness of campaigners' arguments. First you need to establish your legitimacy and demonstrate that it is worth the decision makers' time to listen to you. Only then can you begin serious negotiation. And this negotiation is only partly about persuading decision makers that you are right; often it is more important to show them how taking action will be in their own long-term interests.

Even when decision makers are sympathetic to your arguments and aims, and the relationship is collaborative, encouragement, support, and pressure will be needed, to make sure that they take the actions that you are advocating. Your lobbying can then also become an opportunity to offer detailed advice on implementing the solutions that you are proposing.

In addition to the guidelines given below, see Phase 3 of Part 2 for suggestions on how to develop an influencing strategy.

Relationship-building

It is very rare to achieve your objectives within a single lobbying meeting, even with the best possible preparation. Decision makers often have many different interest groups seeking to influence them; they will also often have fixed views on particular issues. Your overall influencing strategy should include a range of varied ways of reaching decision makers with your messages. This principle applies to lobbying too. Aim to reach a stage where you can establish a dialogue with your key advocacy targets, giving you the opportunity to provide more and more detailed advice, as they come to realise the value of your contributions.

In every meeting with decision makers, you will need to strike a balance between building your relationship with them and negotiating about the issues in question. If the decision makers do not know you at all, you may need to focus mainly on developing the relationship: establishing your credibility and demonstrating that you can offer the decision makers advice that is of interest and potential benefit to them. The early stages of this process will begin before you have a chance to meet: through personal letters, media work, and public support, you should bring your issue (and your organisation) increasingly into their view.

Once you have shown what you have to offer (the strength of public support, the quality of your research, ideas which can help to solve high-profile problems, etc.), you can move forward to detailed negotiations. But even at this stage, do not lose sight of the need to build and maintain good relationships. You may ultimately be seeking to turn the decision makers into champions of your issues and messages, and this will require an on-going dialogue. In each meeting, try to establish an opening for a follow-up meeting (to explore one issue in more detail, or to meet again in three months' time to review progress, for example). You may also seek to expand the lobbying relationship to include other decision makers, by using your supportive target to set up opportunities to lobby others.

Who should lobby?

Should your organisation do the lobbying? Or should you facilitate others to do it? This depends, of course, on your context and the issue, and particularly on who has the best credentials to speak out on the issue. If you are seen as an outsider, or an organisation with foreign links, it may be better to support others to meet the decision makers. But if your organisation is responsible for strong research or has a powerful constituency of public support, you are certainly well placed to do the lobbying yourself. In either case, consider joint lobbying meetings, where you meet a decision maker with three or four representative members of an alliance working on your issue. It provides an opportunity to divide up the roles in the lobbying meeting (see below), as well as providing a range of perspectives and demonstrating a broad-based concern.

See the case study of the UK Working Group on Arms on page 146 for an example of successful joint lobbying.

This section presents a range of practical suggestions to help you to organise and implement your lobbying activity.

Practical guidelines for effective lobbying

The principles outlined below give a general overview of good practice in lobbying. Obviously, the details will depend on your own cultural and political context, and all the suggestions made here will need to be adapted accordingly.

- If you have not previously met the person whom you are lobbying, do some research in advance of the meeting:
  - What is the scope of his or her authority?
  - What action can he or she take?
  - Is there anything in his or her background that is relevant to your objective, or does he or she have any particular interests that may be relevant?
  - Has he or she ever spoken publicly about this issue?
  - What is his or her initial response likely to be: supportive, hostile, or neutral?
  - What do you think he or she already knows about your organisation?
  - Have you had any previous contact, through letters or meetings with officials in his or her team?
  - What is it realistic for you to ask him or her to do?
- Make sure that you communicate the one or two most important messages that you want to convey. Be clear about the objective of the meeting and what action you want as a result.
- Know your subject: make sure that you are fully briefed with up-to-date information.
- If you go as a group, decide who is going to say what. Assign roles: e.g. note taker, introducer, main spokesperson.
- Check in advance that you all understand and agree on the main arguments.
- Be direct and clear, but not confrontational: listen actively and show interest in and understanding of others' point of view.
- Show how and why the decision maker needs to act differently: remember that it is not sufficient simply to win your argument on the issues.
- Plan for different kinds of response: you may have to negotiate compromises.
- If an opportunity arises, mention your key allies and their contribution, in a way that will strengthen their legitimacy to reach this decision maker; allies may be able to achieve a further meeting with this person sooner than you will.
- If appropriate, check what you have agreed before finishing the discussion.
- Leave behind detailed background material (research reports or information on your organisation, for example): they may provide the basis for follow-up with the decision maker's supporting officials, who may have a strong influence on policy formation.
- If possible, get agreement in principle for a follow-up meeting with the decision maker: prepare a clear rationale for this in advance.
- After the meeting, send a letter of thanks to the person for arranging the meeting; summarise what you discussed, and mention any promises that he or she made.
- Keep a summary of the discussion for your own future use.

Negotiating

When you are negotiating, you are in a situation where there is a balance of interests. Several factors influence the nature of the relationship between the two negotiating sides. Decision makers may gain their authority from their formal positions within the government or other organisation; but there will almost always be reasons why you will be able to influence them. Demonstrate the value of your case to them. You might have information that is useful to them, or access to valuable resources, such as local community support. You may be an expert on the issue. If you have links with people who are important to the person with whom you are negotiating (for example, journalists or donor governments), he or she may be more inclined to listen to what you have to say.[2]

The decision maker's perception of your organisation is all-important. Sometimes it is not the power that you actually have but the power that you are believed to have that is important. This explains why the credibility of your own organisation and its links with others is vital.

Choose the right time for the negotiation. Timing can critically affect the perceived importance of your issue. If your meeting follows immediately after a large public demonstration on your issue, for example, you have more power within the negotiation than if the decision maker has seen no evidence of public support.

You should be clear in advance about your 'bottom line' (the minimum that you are prepared to accept) as well as your 'optimum solution' (the ideal solution for you). You should think also about the bottom lines and optimum solutions of the people on the other side of the negotiation. Results tend to be more successful when the two bottom lines overlap.

Negotiating may include bargaining. Don't start by revealing your bottom line. But be prepared to compromise: '*If you start with nothing, demand 100 per cent, then compromise for 30 per cent, you're 30 per cent ahead.*'[3]

And remember that the negotiation does not end at the conclusion of this meeting. Think about how the negotiation is affecting your on-going relationship with this decision maker. If there are unresolved matters, can you leave openings for follow-up? (But beware of deferring a decision that has to be reached now!) Can you agree on partial commitments now, which might be strengthened during future negotiations?

8 Using the media

Most governments and institutions care about their public image. The mass media help to make and shape such images and may therefore be an important tool for you. The media can do the following:

- build awareness and influence public opinion;
- stimulate people to act;
- influence and put pressure on governments and other institutions;
- publicise your work and influence people's perceptions of you.

Engaging the media can enhance your organisation's power, can improve your legitimacy, and may mean the difference between a low-profile activity and a high-impact event commanding significant public interest. The media may also be a highly effective tool for demonstrating public concern for your issue and for changing the minds of decision makers. However, mismanaging your contacts with the media may have disastrous results. In the same way that the media can enhance your profile and legitimacy, they can also destroy it. Understanding how to work with the media, how to develop media strategies, and some of the most basic communications techniques is crucial to making the best use of your media opportunities.

Practical guidelines

The principles outlined below give a general overview of working with the media. The details will need to be adapted according to your particular context.

Understanding how the media work

Monitor your media: who reports on what particular issues, and what perspectives do they promote? The media are rarely neutral on any issue. In relation to any specific medium – a newspaper, or a radio or TV station, for example – find out:

- Who owns it?
- Is it run commercially? Or politically?
- Is it dependent on a political party?
- Is it independent of government?
- Whose politics does it reflect?

- Is it hostile or friendly to you and your concerns?
- What kinds of story does it cover? Are the stories trivial, or trivialised? What kinds of people are they aimed at?

Target audiences

Before deciding which media to use, think about the people whom are you trying to reach, and about how media are used in your culture. For example:

- Who has access to which media in your country?
- Which newspapers, magazines, radio and television programmes most influence public opinion on issues of concern to you?
- Which media do decision makers, politicians, government officials, etc. read, listen to, or watch?
- Which media are most likely to shape the debates on issues of importance to you?
- How important are regional/local media to communities or locally based politicians and decision makers?
- Which journalists particularly influence public opinion or government?
- Is radio more important than print media?
- Are institutions sensitive to media coverage and public opinion in your country?

Case study: using the media to raise public awareness in Malawi

Political liberalisation and civil war in Mozambique, and the disbanding of the youth wing of the former ruling party, all contributed to the problems of the proliferation of small arms in neighbouring Malawi. With democracy came greater elements of lawlessness, an increase in crime, and increased possession of illegal firearms. As a result, there was a growing tendency for people to try to provide for their own security.

In response, the main focus of the Community Safety and Firearms Control Pilot Project in Malawi has been on work with local communities and the police to address the problems of firearms proliferation. Activities included a training of trainers workshop scheme, involving recruits from the Malawi Police Service, NGOs, and community representatives. This was supported by the production and dissemination of a Community Safety Handbook, posters, and a film about community policing, entitled 'Protecting our Lives'.

In addition, the Pilot Project sponsored, funded, and helped to arrange a series of public broadcasts by the Malawi Broadcasting Corporation (MBC) and Television Malawi to promote public awareness of the need to support professional policing to counter armed violence. The MBC and TV Malawi produced four radio and TV programmes on the development of community policing in four districts. In addition, the MBC arranged four panel discussions with senior Malawi police officers and NGO specialists on a range of topics. The programmes were broadcast just before the panel discussions, so that members of the public could ask questions and express their opinions to the panellists for on-air discussion.

During site recordings, posters, leaflets, and audiocassettes on themes related to human rights and firearms control were distributed to members of the local communities.

The aims of this media work were to improve the awareness of the general public in Malawi about the work of the police and especially of the need for community support to counter violent crime and the spread of firearms.

A later evaluation showed that, following the broadcasts, there were indicators of changed attitudes on the part of both police and local people in relation to the work of community policing. In Mchinji and Mangochi districts, for example, the local community had helped the police to recover stolen goods and a number of small arms after the airing of the programme. In Dedza, crime-prevention committees were being established as a result of the radio programme.

The radio programmes were felt to be one starting point for the debates on tackling the issues of violent crime and firearms control.

[This case study has been developed by the Community Safety and Firearms Control Pilot in Malawi and is based on their experiences and opinions.]

Working with the media

Three things are vital to your relationship with the media: credibility, immediacy, and timing. Analysis of examples of good practice suggests the following guidelines.

- Resist the temptation to try to get as much coverage as you can: you should build your media activity around a media strategy, using those media that will genuinely help to achieve your objectives.
- Provide information to journalists in a ready-to-use format: the more you do this, the more you are likely to control what they say.

- Build good long-term relationships with journalists, especially by fostering informal links.
- Keep an up-to-date list of media contacts.
- Be aware of the journalists' agenda, not just your own agenda.
- Develop a reactive strategy: how will you respond to criticisms or unfortunate events? How will you react when there is a positive news story?

What the media want[4]

Normally the media will be more interested in a story which

- affects people
- is happening now
- is here
- is different
- inspires an emotional response
- has celebrity interest
- is 'the most ...' (the biggest, the newest, the fastest, the first, etc.).

Developing media lists[5]

Develop a list of contacts, and keep it up to date. Keep files of press clippings and add to the list when new reporters cover your stories.

Think about people in the following positions:

- radio news directors and reporters
- television news editors, reporters, and producers
- wire-service bureau chiefs and day-book editors
- newspaper editors, news reporters, defence/security reporters, columnists, editors of op/ed (opinion/editorial) pages, features editors
- talk-show producers and bookers (those who arrange the guest speakers)
- editors of community or special-interest newspapers and magazines
- diary editors on newspapers/radio/wire service/television.

Techniques for working with the media

The media release

- Use headed paper, with printed details of your organisation's name and address.
- Always include at least one contact name, with a telephone number and/or an email address.
- Keep it short and simple. Ideally, media releases should be confined to one side of one sheet of paper.

- Always put a date on your news release. Make it clear to whom it is addressed and when the embargo time is. If it is not embargoed, put 'For immediate release'.
- Make the heading and first sentence sound interesting.
- Put the main facts in the first paragraph, if possible.
- When promoting a special event, make sure that you include all the following information: **Who** is doing it? **What** is happening? **Where** is it happening? **When** is it happening? **Why** is it happening?
- Try to include a good quote.

The media conference

A media conference usually consists of someone making a short speech and then answering questions and being available for follow-up interviews.

- Use this tool sparingly – only when you have a major news story to announce and/or someone in whom the media are interested.
- Consider holding a joint press conference with other organisations.
- Keep the panel small and the speeches short.
- Remember that various types of media have differing needs.

The media pack

At the launch of a major campaign or research report, it may be useful to provide a media pack which summarises the key information. This might include, for example,

- summaries of the major findings or issues of the report
- outlines of some of the individual cases featured in the report
- sample quotes from the report
- a list of the major recommendations
- what you hope to achieve, and what will be happening
- anticipated questions and answers: this is a good way to provide clarification on controversial or complex issues.

Interviews

The key to doing good interviews is a thorough knowledge of your subject and good preparation.

Before the interview

- Agree the time, the place, and the duration.
- Agree the subject and define the issues with the producer or interviewer. Be specific about the topics to be covered.
- Make a list of the three or four most important points you want to make. Express them as 'sound-bites' (short, dramatic statements).

- For radio and TV: research the programme: who is the audience? Is the show live or pre-recorded? Is it a discussion?
- Anticipate the questions and practise your answers; rehearse stories that illustrate your key points.
- Check that you have the latest information.
- For radio and TV: discuss with the journalist the questions to be asked first.

During the interview

- Try to relax.
- Keep your answers concise; use simple language and avoid jargon.
- Do not get side-tracked. Keep your key points in mind, and continually steer the conversation back to them.
- Do not allow a journalist to put words in your mouth.
- Use examples and stories to illustrate facts and statistics.
- Stay calm, but don't be afraid to show some emotion. If you are attacked by a hostile question, you should not get upset: just answer back firmly.
- For radio and TV: do not fidget. Cameras and microphones pick up the slightest movement.
- For radio and TV: do not interrupt or speak at the same time as others.
- For TV: remember that the camera is on you at all times.
- Most important of all: remember that **nothing is ever 'off the record'**: say nothing that you would not be happy to see in print, or heard broadcast to the public.

Feature articles

- For a major report, negotiate with one or more newspapers to carry a feature article to reinforce the news coverage. Features provide an opportunity to elaborate an issue in depth, using stories and more detailed analysis.
- Newspapers often have an op/ed (opinion/editorial) page to allow substantial space for opinion pieces.

Letters and phone-in programmes

The letters pages of newspapers provide a forum for encouraging discussion of issues and demonstrating public interest and concern.

- Keep your contribution short.
- Make it a response to something that has been in the news.
- Have letters signed by someone representing an organisation.

- Provide a contact number so that facts can be checked.
- Radio phone-in programmes which invite audience participation provide an opportunity to demonstrate concern or express interest about an issue. Even if the topic is not precisely relevant to your issue, you can often use a story to create a link between the two.

Photographs and photo opportunities

- Ensure maximum visual impact, for example by using a celebrity, and/or an eye-catching public event.
- Give the media plenty of notice. Be clear about the location and timing. Send out a media release giving these details and headed 'photo opportunity'.
- Be flexible if possible. Offer to rehearse or re-stage events to fit in with the schedule of the newspaper.
- Take your own photographs and offer them to newspapers that did not send their own photographers.
- Add captions to relate the picture to your issue, and to explain who is doing what, why, where, and when.

9 Taking action: a summary

Effective action involves combining your experience, skills, and legitimacy with those of your allies to create change. Your chosen method of doing this – through media, lobbying, mass action, etc. – will depend on what you want to achieve, and on the position from which you are starting. A membership organisation will be better suited to mass letter writing than a policy organisation, for example: the latter would be better placed to develop public-policy recommendations with government officials. Usually a combination of two or more approaches or actions is most effective, especially if it is co-ordinated with the work of others with similar goals.

It is important to understand that often change is a long and complex process. It involves developing relationships – sometimes over considerable periods of time – and it involves a lot of hard work: understanding problems, conducting research, developing messages, and delivering these messages to those with the power to make the change that you desire.

Change does not always occur in expected ways and in accordance with your strategies and plans. It is important always to think of the wider context in which your action is taking place, and remember that sometimes if you are not progressing it might not be your research or action that is wrong, but the focus of your efforts. For example, you might be lobbying the government in your country for stronger national legislation on arms exports. You may be failing to bring about change because – although it agrees that there is a need for more stringent arms-exports legislation – the government does not want to do something that would put commercial activity in your country at a disadvantage. However, if you broaden the context and focus on the development of regional legislation, then your government might be less hostile – if, for example in this case, it could be demonstrated that the commercial *status quo* would not be altered. In some cases it is possible that the government might become a positive advocate of your case.

There is no perfect way to plan or to act. Often changes happen as a result of political, social, and economic factors combining in a way that you cannot anticipate or control. The forces resisting change are often extremely powerful, and your resources may be scarce. However, there are many examples, included in this handbook and elsewhere, which prove that change is possible.

A thorough approach to planning will help you to select the most appropriate ways in which to act for change. And a detailed understanding of the various options for taking action will help you to select the right approach at the right time. The contents of this handbook provide a framework for helping you to plan and act effectively. In the end, however, your success will depend on a combination of what happens in the wider world and your own skills, dedication, and passion.

> *'Vision without action achieves nothing.*
> *Action without vision just passes the time.*
> *Vision with action can change the world.'*
> (Nelson Mandela)

Part 4

Contacts

This part of the handbook contains addresses of groups and agencies that have contributed significantly to the development of the book, who may be able to give you further information and support in your action against the abuse of small arms. The International Action Network on Small Arms is a good place to try first, so it appears first on the list. All other organisations are presented in alphabetical order.

International Action Network on Small Arms – IANSA
PO Box 422
37 Store Street
London
WC1E 7QF
UK
www.iansa.org
Tel: +44 (0) 20 7953 7626
Contact: Sally Joss

Africa Peace Forum/International Resource Group
PO Box 76621
Nairobi 508
KENYA
www.aminiafrika.org
kilenem@afrionline.co.ke
Tel: +254 (20) 574 092
Fax: +254 (20) 561 357
Contact: Ochieng Adala

American Friends Service Committee
1501 Cherry Street
Philadelphia
PA 19102
UNITED STATES
www.afsc.org/
Tel: +1 (215) 241-7000
Fax: +1 (215) 241-7275

Amnesty International, International Secretariat
1 Easton Street
London
WC1X ODW
UK
www.amnesty.org
amnestyis@amnesty.org
Tel: +44 (0)207 4135500
Please contact the International Secretariat for information on Amnesty International's offices in other countries

The Arias Foundation for Peace and Human Progress
Apartado 8-6410-1000
San José
Costa Rica
www.arias.or.cr
Tel: (506) 255-2955
Fax: (506) 255-2244

Bonn International Centre for Conversion (BICC)
An der Eliasbethkirche 25
Bonn NRW 53113
GERMANY
www.disarmament.de
Tel: +49 228 911960
Fax: +49 228 241215
Contact: Sami Faltas

British American Security Information Council (BASIC)
Lafone House
11-13 Leathermarket Street
London SE1 3HW
UK
Tel: +44 (0)20 74070 2977
Fax: +44 (0)20 7407 2988
www.basicint.org
Contact: Ian Davis

Centre for Democratic Empowerment
BP 397
Abidjan 06
COTE D'IVOIRE
Cede-reg@afnet.net
Tel: +255 22 41 14 21
Fax: +255 22 44 98 87
Contact: Conmany Wesseh

Community Safety and Firearms Control Pilot
Public Affairs Committee
P/B B-348
Lilongwe 3
MALAWI
Tel: +265 1 772 696
Fax: +265 1 772 696
Contact: Robert Phrir

Conscientious Objectors in Bosnia & Herzegovina (COIB)
Dzemala Bijedica 309
71000 Sarajevo
BOSNIA & HERZEGOVINA
Tel: +38761205546
Fax: +38733627415
Contact: Darko Brkan

Federation of American Scientists Arms Sales Monitoring Project
1717 K Street NW
Suite 209
Washington DC 20036
USA
www.fas.org/asmp
Tel: +1 202/546-3300

Forumi i Iniciativs Qytetare (FIQ)
Epopeja e Jezercit
Ferizaj
KOSOVO
fiqfer@hotmail.com
Tel: +377 44 155370
Fax: +381 29 028900

Foundation for Security and Development in Africa (FOSDA)
PO Box 3140 Cantonment
Accra
GHANA
fosda@africanus.net
Tel: + 233 (21) 811 291
Fax: +233 (21) 811 322
Contact: Afi Yakubu

Human Rights Watch, Arms Division
1630 Connecticut Avenue, N.W.
Suite 500
Washington DC 20009
USA
www.hrw.org/arms/index.php
Tel: +1 (202) 612 4321
Fax: +1 (202) 612 4333

Institute of Security Studies
PO Box 1787
Brooklyn Square
Pretoria 0075
SOUTH AFRICA
www.iss.co.za
Tel :+ 27 12 346 9500/2
Fax: + 27 12 460 0998

Institute of War and Peace Reporting
Lancaster House
33 Islington High Street
London N1 9LH
UK
www.iwpr.net
Tel: +44 207 713 7130
Fax: + 44 207 713 7140

International Alert
346 Clapham Road
London SW9 9AP
UK
www.international-alert.org
www.womenbuildingpeace.org
Tel +44 (0) 20 7627 6800
Fax +44 (0) 20 7627 6900
Contact: Helena Vazquez

International Campaign to Ban Landmines
110 Maryland Avenue NE
Box 6, Suite 509
Washington DC 20002
USA
www.icbl.org
Tel: +1 202 547 2667

International Committee of the Red Cross and Red Crescent (ICRC)
19 avenue de la Paix
CH 1202 Geneva
SWITZERLAND
www.icrc.org

International Physicians for the Prevention of Nuclear War – IPPNW
27 Massachusetts Avenue
Cambridge
MA 029139
UNITED STATES
www.ippnw.org/SmallArmsStart.html

Kibera Youth Programme for Peace and Development
PO Box 10805
Nairobi 100
KENYA
kenodhiss@yahoo.com
Tel: +254 (20) 577 557/8
Fax: +254 (20) 577 557
Contact: Kennedy Odhiambo

MALAO
BP 5142
Dakar-Fann
SENEGAL
Tel: +221 824 0933
Fax: +221 825 5654

Norwegian Initiative on Small Arms Transfers – NISAT
c/o International Peace Research Institute
Fuglehauggata 11
NO-0260 Oslo
NORWAY
www.nisat.org
Tel: +47 (22) 54 7700
Fax: +47 (22) 54 7701
Contact: Nicholas Marsh

Oxfam GB
Conflict Campaign Team
Suite 20
266 Banbury Road
Oxford
OX2 7DL
UK
www.oxfaminternational.org
Tel: + 44 1865 311311
Contact: Oliver Sprague (who can supply details of Oxfam's offices in other countries)

Pastoralist Peace and Development Initiative (PPDI)
Jihan Centre
PO Box 838
Garissa
North Eastern Province
KENYA

SaferAfrica
Trelawney House
173 Beckett Street
Arcadia
Pretoria SA
SOUTH AFRICA
Tel: +27 12 3446701
Fax: +27 12 3446708
www.saferafrica.org
Contact: Virginia Gamba

Saferworld
46 Grosvenor Gardens
London SW1W 0EB
UK
Tel. +44 (0) 20 7881 9293
Fax. +44 (0) 20 7881 9291
www.saferworld.org.uk
Contact: Henry Smith

Security Research & Information Centre (SRIC)
PO Box 56622
Nairobi
Westlands 200
KENYA
sric@africaonline.co.ke
Tel: +254 (20) 444 9503
Fax: +254 (20) 444 8903
Contact: Lt Col Jan Kamenju

Serbia and Montenegro Red Cross
11 000 Belgrade
Simina 19
SERBIA AND MONTENEGRO
www.jck.org.yu/
Tel: + 381 11 623564
Fax: + 381 11 622965

Slovak Working Group on Arms Trade
Dept of Political Science
Comenius University
Gondova 2
Bratislava 81103
SLOVAKIA
Tel: +421 908 416 679
Contact: Vladimir Lefik

Small Arms Survey
Avenue Blanc 47
1202 Geneva
SWITZERLAND
www.smallarmssurvey.org
Tel. + 41 22 908.57.77
Fax. + 41 22 732.27.38

South Asia Partnership International
571/15 Galle Road
Colombo 6
SRI LANKA
www.eureka.lk/sapint
sapi@eureka.lk
Tel: +94 (1) 507 009
Fax: +94 (75) 514 587
Contact: Dr James Arputharaj Williams

South Eastern Europe Clearing House for the Control of Small Arms and Light Weapons (SEESAC)
Jnska Veselinovica 13
Belgrade
Serbia 11000
SERBIA AND MONTENEGRO
Tel: +381 11 444 2902
Fax: +381 11 454 351
www.undp.org.yu/seesac
Contact: Simon Rynn

Stockholm International Peace Research Institute (SIPRI)
Signalistgatan 9
SE-169 70 Solna
SWEDEN
www.sipri.org
Tel: +46 (8) 655 9736
Contact: Peter Wiezman

UK Working Group on Arms (UKWG)
Amnesty International
BASIC
Christian Aid
International Alert
Oxfam GB
Saferworld
Contact through Saferworld

United Nations Department of Disarmament Affairs (UNDDA)
Room S-3170
United Nations
New York
NY 10017
USA
disarmament.un.org/gender.htm

United Nations Development Programme (UNDP)
One United Nations Plaza
New York
NY 10017
USA
www.undp.org/
Tel: +1 (212) 906-5558
Fax: +1 (212) 906-5364
Contact the New York office for details of UNDP offices in other countries

United Nations High Commissioner on Human Rights (UNHCHR)
8-14 Avenue de la Paix
1211 Geneva 10
SWITZERLAND
Tel: +41 22 917 9000

United Nations Institute for Disarmament Research (UNDIR)
Palais des Nations
Geneva CH 1211
SWITZERLAND
Tel +41 (22) 917 3186
Fax: +41 (22) 917 0176
www.unidir.org
Contact: Patricia Lewis

Viva Rio
Ladiera de Gloria, 98
Rio de Janeiro
RJ 2-211-120
BRAZIL
www.vivario.org.br
Tel: +55 (21) 2555 3750
Fax: + 55 (21) 2558 1381

Working Group for Weapons Reduction (WGWR)
c/o AFSC
PO Box 604
Phnom Penh
CAMBODIA
www.wgwr.org
Tel: +855 (23) 216 400
Fax: +855 (23) 213 447
Contact: Sinthay Neb

The World Health Organisation's Injuries and Violence Prevention Department
20 Avenue Appia
1211 Geneva 27
SWITZERLAND
www5.who.int/violence_injury_prevention/main.cfm?p=0000000160
Tel: + 41 22 791 2111
Fax: + 41 22 791 3111

Notes

Preface

1 Speech to the Humanitarian Coalition conference, November 2001, by Isaac Lappia.

2 Statement by UN Secretary General, Kofi Annan, to the UN Conference on the Illicit Trade in Small Arms and Light Weapons in All Its Aspects, 9 July 2001.

3 *Small Arms Survey 2002*, Oxford University Press.

4 Forecast International, 2002, cited in *Small Arms Survey 2002*, Oxford University Press, p. 14.

5 Ibid.

Part 1

1 1997 *Report of the UN Panel of Governmental Experts on Small Arms*, United Nations, A/52/298, 27 August 1997.

2 'Counting the Human Cost', *Small Arms Survey 2002*, A Project of the Graduate Institute of International Studies, Oxford: Oxford University Press.

3 Ibid.

4 Ibid.

5 This section has been compiled using the following sources: 'Profiling the Problem', *Small Arms Survey 2001*, A Project of the Graduate Institute of International Studies, Oxford: Oxford University Press; 'Counting the Human Cost', *Small Arms Survey 2002*, A Project of the Graduate Institute of International Studies, Oxford: Oxford University Press; *Combating the Illicit Trade in Small Arms and Light Weapons: enhancing controls on legal transfers*, Biting the Bullet Briefing 6, BASIC, Saferworld, and International Alert, 2001; *What is Legal? What is Illegal?* Emanuela Gillard, Lauterpacht Research Centre for International Law, Cambridge; available on-line at www.international-alert.org/publications.htm

6 Report of the UN Disarmament Commission, *Guidelines for International Arms Transfers in the Context of General Assembly Resolution 46/36 of 6th December 1991*, UN Doc. A/51/42, 22 May 1996, Annex 1 para. 6.

7 Extracted and summarised from a Working Paper to the UN Sub Commission on the Promotion and Protection of Human Rights by Barbara Frey. E/CN.4/Sub.2/2002/39, 30 May 2002.

8 *1997 Report of the UN Panel of Governmental Experts on Small Arms* op. cit., para 14.

9 Ibid., para. 17.

10 See, for example, B. Pirseyedi, 'The Small Arms Problem in Central Asia: Features and Implications', UNIDIR May 2000; United Nations, *The Machel Review 1996–2000: A Critical Analysis of Progress Made and Obstacles Encountered in Increasing Protection for War-Affected Children*, United Nations, 2000, p. 34 (hereinafter, *The Machel Review*).

11 Robert Muggah and Eric Berman, 'Humanitarianism Under Threat: the Humanitarian Impacts of Small Arms and Light Weapons' (*Small Arms Survey, 2001*), pp. 3-4. In this study, commissioned by the Reference Group on Small Arms of the United Nations Inter-Agency Standing Committee, the researchers found that in the cases of Colombia, East Timor, and

Kenya, forced displacement is influenced by even a subjective perception of firearms-related violence.

12 Kathi Austin, 'Armed Refugee Camps as a Microcosm of the Link between Arms Availability and Insecurity', 2002, p.1. Unpublished paper available from the author: a case study of arms flows, availability, and impacts associated with the Dadaab refugee camps in north-eastern Kenya.

13 *Arms Availability and the Situation of Civilians in Armed Conflict*, International Committee of the Red Cross, Geneva 1999, p. 16 (citing Kuzman study) (hereinafter 'ICRC Arms Availability Report').

14 Ibid.

15 Robin M. Coupland and David R. Meddings, 'Mortality associated with use of weapons in armed conflicts, wartime atrocities, and civilian mass shootings: literature review', *British Medical Journal*, 1999, Vol. 319, pp. 407-10.

16 Peter Salama, Bruce Laurence, and Monica Nolan, 'Health and human rights in contemporary humanitarian crises: is Kosovo more important than Sierra Leone?', *British Medical Journal*, 1999, Vol. 319, pp. 1569-71.

17 United Nations, Report of the Secretary-General on the Protection of Civilians in Armed Conflict (S/1999/957), para. 16.

18 *The Machel Review*, op. cit., p. 5.

19 Ibid., p. 33. An RPG is an anti-tank grenade launcher.

20 Robert Muggah, 'Caught in the crosshairs: the humanitarian impact of small arms', draft chapter for *Small Arms Survey, 2002*, p. 9.

21 Robert Muggah and Eric Berman, 'Humanitarianism under threat', *Small Arms Survey, 2001*, pp. 4-5. The UN does not collect statistics on injuries directly resulting from armed violence.

22 Amnesty International, 'Human Rights Abuses with Small Arms, Illustrative cases from Amnesty International reports 2000–2001'.

23 *Arms Sales Monitor*, August 2002, Federation of American Scientists.

24 'Country Reports on Human Rights Practices 2000', US State Department, released by the Bureau of Democracy, Human Rights and Labor, February 2001.

25 See, for example, *The Terror Trade Times 2002*, Amnesty International.

26 Ibid.

27 Michael Freeman, 'Small arms in Africa: counting the cost of gun violence', *Africa Recovery*, Vol. 15 No. 4, December 2001, p. 1.

28 Virginia Gamba, quoted in Carolyn Dempster: 'Guns, gangs and culture of violence', BBC News, 10 April 2002.

29 Wendy Cukier, *Combating the Illicit Trade in Small Arms and Light Weapons: Strengthening Domestic Regulations*, Biting the Bullet Briefing 7, BASIC, Saferworld, and International Alert, p.7, 2001. Available on-line at www.international-alert.org/publications.htm

30 Paul Eavis, 'The hidden security threat: transnational organised crime activity', *RUSI Journal*, December 2001, Vol. 146, No. 6.

31 World Health Organisation, *Small Arms and Global Health*, Geneva, 2001, http://www5.who.int/violence_injury_prevention/download.cfm?id=0000000158

32 Wendy Cukier, op. cit., p.6.

33 Eavis, op.cit.

34 'Government response to gun crime in the UK needs to go further', press release, Saferworld, 9 January 2003.

35 For more detail, see D. Darchiasvili: 'Georgia: a hostage to arms' in *The Caucasus: Armed and Defended* Saferworld, 2003.

36 Luke Downing, 'Child Combatants in Organised Armed Violence', ISER and Viva Rio, www.desarme.org/

37 Michael Fleshman, 'Small arms in Africa: counting the cost of gun violence', *Africa Recovery*, December 2001, Vol. 15, No. 4, p.1.

38 S. Gautam and T. Koirala (eds.), *Women and Children in the Periphery of People's War*, Institute of Human Rights Communication in Nepal, December 2001.

39 International Committee of the Red Cross, *Small Arms Survey, 2002.*

40 Human Rights Watch, World Report 2002.

41 Findings of a report by Working Group for Weapons Reduction in Cambodia, 1994.

42 Human Rights Watch, World Report 1996.

43 See, for example, Report of UN Panel of Governmental Experts on Small Arms, UN Document Reference A/52/298, 1997.

44 K. Mkutu, 'Pastoralism and Conflict in the Horn of Africa', Saferworld/University of Bradford, December 2001.

45 D. Bannerjee and R. Muggah (eds.), *Small Arms and Human Insecurity*, RCSS/SAS, Colombo, 2002.

46 'Arms Availability and the Situation of Civilians in Armed Conflict', ICRC, Geneva, 1999.

47 United Nations, 'International Study on Firearms Regulation', UN, New York, 1998.

48 P. Cook and J. Ludwig, 'Guns in America: National Survey on Private Ownership and Use of Firearms', National Institute of Justice Research Brief, US Department of Justice, Washington DC, 1997.

49 M. Buvinic and A. Morrison, 'Violence as an Obstacle to Development', Inter-American Development Bank, Washington DC 1999, quoted in E. Krug, L. Dahlberg, J. Mercy, A Zwi and R. Lozano (eds.), *World Report on Violence and Health*, World Health Organisation, Geneva, 2002.

50 Elizabeth Clegg, Sami Faltas, Glenn McDonald and Camilla Waszink, *Reducing the Stock of the Illicit Trade: Promoting Best Practice in Weapons Collection Programmes*, Biting the Bullet Briefing 12, BASIC, Saferworld and International Alert, p.6, 2001. Available on-line at www.international-alert.org/publications.htm

51 Ibid., p.7.

52 See, for example, UNIDIR Disarmament and Conflict Resolution Project series on Managing Arms in Peace Processes, UNIDIR, Geneva, 1995-1998.

53 Wulf Paes, 'Weapons Collection Programmes: Different Approaches and Lessons in Practical Disarmament', conference paper, given at 'Enhancing Security in the Balkans: Enacting the Stability Pact Regional Implementation Plan on Small Arms', 24-25 June 2002, Belgrade.

54 Henny J. van der Graaf and Sami Faltas (2001) 'Weapons in exchange for development: an innovative approach to the collection of weapons in Albania', in Sami Faltas and Joseph Di Chiaro III (eds.), *Managing the Remnants of War: Micro-disarmament as an Element of Peace-building*, pp. 159-82.

55 Amnesty International, Brazil Country Report, Annual Report 2001, available on-line at www.amnesty.org

56 Owen Greene, *Stockpiling Security and Reducing Surplus Weapons*, Biting the Bullet Briefing 3, p.6, 2001. Available on-line at www.international-alert.org/publications.htm

57 Ibid.

58 Ibid., p.7.

59 Ibid., p.10.

60 UN Disarmament Commission, op. cit., para. 17.

61 Section II, Paragraph 11 of the Programme of Action to Prevent, Combat and Eradicate the Illicit Trade in Small Arms and Light Weapons in All its Aspects.

62 Amnesty International, The American Friends Service Committee, The Arias Foundation for Peace and Human Progress, BASIC, the Federation of American Scientists, the Friends Committee on National Legislation, Oxfam, Project Ploughshares, and Saferworld.

63 The complete text of the proposed agreement is available at www.armslaw.org .

64 American Friends Service Committee, Amnesty International, Oscar Arias, Norman Borlaug, His Holiness the Dalai Lama, John Hume, International Physicians for the Prevention of Nuclear War, Mairead Maguire, Rigoberta Menchu, Adolfo Perez Esquivel, Jose Ramos Horta, Joseph Rotblat, Aung San Suu Kyi, the Reverend Desmond Tutu, Lech Walesa, Elie Wiesel, Betty Williams, and Jody Williams.

65 Report of the Panel of Experts on Violations of Security Council Sanctions against UNITA. UN Document S/2000/203, annex 1. 10 March 2000. Final Report of the Monitoring Mechanism on Angola Sanctions, UN document S/2000/1225, Annex. 21 December 2000.

66 Wendy Cukier, op.cit., p.2.

67 Ibid.

68 1996 Inter-American Convention Against the Illicit Manufacturing of and Trafficking in Firearms, Ammunition, Explosives, and Other Related Materials (OAS Convention); 1991 Firearms Directive, Council Directive 91/477/EEC of 18 June 1991 on the control of the acquisition and possession of weapons; UN Convention on Transnational Organised Crime of 2001; Resolution 1209 of the UN Security Council, November 1998; UN General Assembly Declaration of December 1999; UN Commission on Crime Prevention and Criminal Justice Resolution of 1997.

69 See Human Rights Watch open letter to the President of Burkina Faso, 28 March 2000, at www.hrw.org/press/2000/03/burkina0330letter.htm.

70 Those States that have ratified so far are Antigua and Barbuda (2003), Argentina (2001), Bahamas (1998), Belize (1997), Bolivia (1999), Brazil (1999), Colombia (2003), Costa Rica (2000), Ecuador (1999), El Salvador (1999), Grenada (2002), Guatemala (2003), Mexico (1998), Nicaragua (1999), Panama (1999), Paraguay (2000), Peru (1999), Uruguay (2001), and Venezuela (2002).

71 OSCE Member States are Albania, Andorra, Armenia, Austria, Azerbaijan, Belarus, Belgium, Bosnia and Herzegovina, Bulgaria, Canada, Croatia, Cyprus, Czech Republic, Denmark, Estonia, Finland, France, Georgia, Germany, Greece, Holy See, Hungary, Iceland, Ireland, Italy, Kazakhstan, Kyrgyzstan, Latvia, Liechtenstein, Lithuania, Luxembourg, Malta, Moldova, Monaco, Netherlands, Norway, Poland, Portugal, Romania, Russian Federation, San Marino, Serbia and Montenegro, Slovak Republic, Slovenia, Spain, Sweden, Switzerland, Tajikistan, The former Yugoslav Republic of Macedonia, Turkey, Turkmenistan, Ukraine, United Kingdom, United States of America, and Uzbekistan.

72 Elizabeth Clegg, Owen Greene, Sarah Meek, and Geraldine O'Callaghan, *Regional Initiatives and the 2001 UN Conference: Building Mutual Support and Complementarity*, Biting the Bullet Briefing 2, BASIC, Saferworld, and International Alert, p.39, 2001. Available on-line at www.international-alert.org/publications.htm

73 The principles include, inter alia, that 'the participating States reaffirm', for example, 'the need to ensure that arms transferred are not used in violation of the purposes and principles of the Charter of the United Nations'. Also, 'each participating State will, in considering proposed transfers, take into account', for instance: (i) the respect for human rights and fundamental freedoms in the recipient country; (ii) the internal and regional situation in and around the recipient country, in the light of existing tensions or armed conflicts.

74 OSCE Document on Small Arms and Light Weapons, 24 November 2000.

75 Michael Crowley, Roy Isbister, and Sarah Meek, *Building Comprehensive Controls on Small Arms Manufacturing, Transfer and End-Use*, Biting the Bullet Briefing 13, BASIC, Saferworld, and International Alert, p.15, 2001. Available on-line at www.international-alert.org/publications.htm

76 Existing EU members: Austria, Belgium, Denmark, Finland, France, Germany, Greece, Ireland, Italy, Luxembourg, Netherlands, Portugal, Spain, Sweden, and the UK. Associate states due to become full EU members in May 2004: Cyprus, Czech Republic, Estonia, Hungary, Latvia, Lithuania, Malta, Poland, Slovak Republic, and Slovenia.

Part 2

1 Notes in this section have been summarised and adapted from Oxfam's *Gender Training Manual*, pp. 18-37.

2 See *Advocacy Sourcebook*, by Valerie Miller and Jane Covey (Institute of Development Research, 1997), for further exploration of issues of legitimacy, credibility, and accountability.

3 This analysis is based on comments in Don Hubert's *The Landmine Ban: A Case Study in Humanitarian Advocacy*, Thomas J Watson Jr Institute for International Studies, Occasional Paper 42 (2000).

4 Adapted from *Impact Assessment for Development Agencies*, by Chris Roche, Oxford: Oxfam (1999).

5 Adapted from Mark Lattimer's *Campaigning Handbook*, 2nd edition, Directory of Social Change (2000).

Part 3

1 Adapted from risk-assessment procedures used by Amnesty International.

2 For a more detailed exploration of issues of power and influence, see Charles Handy's *Understanding Organizations*, fourth edition, Penguin Books (1993).

3 Quotation from Saul D. Alinsky, *Rules for Radicals*, p.59, Vintage Books Edition (1989).

4 From www.greenpeace.org.au/getactive

5 From 'So you want to publicise your campaign?' in ICBL's Campaign Kit, available at www.icbl.org

Index

Notes

The use of italics denotes figures and tables.
B after a page number indicates material in a box, e.g. 13B.
CS after a page number indicates a Case Study, e.g. 112CS.

www.ingramcontent.com/pod-product-compliance
Lightning Source LLC
Chambersburg PA
CBHW041101050426
42334CB00064B/3287
* 9 7 8 0 8 5 5 9 8 4 9 7 7 *